Truth and Community

DIVERSITY AND ITS LIMITS IN THE ECUMENICAL MOVEMENT

by

Michael Kinnamon

WILLIAM B. EERDMANS PUBLISHING COMPANY

GRAND RAPIDS, MICHIGAN

WCC PUBLICATIONS

GENEVA

Copyright © 1988 by Wm. B. Eerdmans Publishing Co.
255 Jefferson Ave. S.E., Grand Rapids, Mich. 49503

First published 1988 jointly by Eerdmans and WCC Publications,
P.O. Box 66, 1211 Geneva 20, Switzerland.

Library of Congress Cataloging-in-Publication Data

Kinnamon, Michael.
Truth and community.
1. Christian union.
2. Religious pluralism—Christianity.
I. Title.
BX8.2.K47 1988   262'.0011   88-6953
Eerdmans ISBN 0-8028-0327-X
WCC ISBN 2-8254-0935-9

Contents

v

PREFACE

The main thesis of this book is that the vision behind the modern ecumenical movement involves a necessary tension between truth and diverse community, and that the central question facing the ecumenical movement is, therefore, how to determine the limits of acceptable diversity. This thesis is by no means new (although my presentation of it may be), but it has been frequently violated, forgotten, or ignored.

Many Christians who identify themselves as "evangelical" seem to take it as a given that the ecumenically involved churches skate far too lightly over varying claims to truth in their pursuit of visible unity. Unfortunately, this suspicion is sometimes reinforced by ecumenical enthusiasts who make it sound as if there are no legitimate limits to the diversity that the church should encompass.

But conservative evangelicals are certainly not the only ones who weight the tension heavily in favor of "truth." While diversity is increasingly acknowledged to be a necessary—indeed, desirable—aspect of efforts to achieve doctrinal reconciliation, there is also an increasing tendency in other parts of the ecumenical movement to constrict the circle of acceptable diversity with regard to social-political commitments. This has contributed to an unfortunate bifurcation of the ecumenical agenda. Some seem to fear that the search for one eucharistic fellowship among people who confess that Jesus Christ is Lord can detract from the urgent need for prophetic witness against those (including Christians) whose actions perpetuate injustice. Others seem to fear that the church's political involvements against the evils of history are at times unnecessarily divisive and thus detrimental to its role as eucharistic community and witness to the gospel.

Even more disturbing, laypersons (and clergy, for that matter) who desire to be ecumenical are often unable to identify dialogue with truth, or unity with commitment. "I know it's good to be 'tolerant,'" I sometimes hear, "but it's hard to speak persuasively about the truth of the gospel when you are so open to other perspectives." This inability to see ecumenism as a tension involving both truth and diverse community bolsters Dean Kelley's well-known hypothesis that "social strength and leniency do not seem to go together"—in other words, that an ecumenical church is unlikely to grow and be dynamic.

These concerns indicate the audiences I hope to address. First, it is my sincere hope that the book will find readers among evangelical Christians who have previously avoided ecumenical dialogue, perhaps because of their commitment to the importance of truth or "purity." Such readers may well disagree with much that I have to say but still find the argument a useful framework for further discussion. Second, I hope that the book will spark among those already deeply involved in the ecumenical movement some debate on how to articulate a more integrated vision of what that movement is about. Finally, I think the most important audiences are pastors, who may find this a useful text for teaching about ecumenism, and laypersons, who may see more clearly that ecumenism is not simply a movement for theologians and church leaders but a worldview rooted firmly in the gospel and especially appropriate for our troubled times.

I am convinced that with God's guidance it is possible—indeed, essential—for the church to reject the pretensions of Caesar while still humbly acknowledging that its hold on truth is not absolute. It is possible—essential—for the church to be an inclusive community of diverse groups—Protestant, Catholic, and Orthodox, black and white, liberal and conservative, Russian and American, male and female— while still drawing firm lines against apartheid and other examples of lovelessness, or against allegiance to lesser gods. The fact that our churches so often split these concerns—parochialism and idolatry, diversity and truth—indicates how little the ecumenical vision is understood. And, without a proper understanding, it is no wonder that ecumenism is low on many of our churches' lists of priorities, something they pay lip service to while their passion lies elsewhere.

The following pages are not intended to be a history of ecumenical thought or a summary of current thinking in the ecumenical movement—although I draw heavily on both. Rather, I am arguing a case for what ecumenism, in my opinion, should be (and, indeed, what it has been at its best). The first two chapters set forth the basic argument and suggest several theological principles on which ecumenism is founded. The middle three chapters explore how the ecumenical movement has determined (explicitly or implicitly) the limits of acceptable diversity on doctrinal, social, and confessional issues. The last two chapters chart future directions, suggest two principles for guiding the church as it probes the limits of diversity, and offer a personal understanding of the "ecumenical worldview." The argument presented is not simple, but I have tried to be straightforward in order to make the book accessible to interested laypersons. Many sections contain numbered lists of propositions or observations to make the argument easier to follow.

Parts of the following chapters have been presented to ecumenical conferences—involving clergy, laity, and professional ecumenists—around the country. My thinking has been greatly stimulated by the discussions at these meetings. I must also express appreciation to my colleagues, past and present, at the World Council of Churches, the Council on Christian Unity of the Christian Church (Disciples of Christ), and the Christian Theological Seminary. Special thanks is due to Robert Welsh, my frequent collaborator on ecumenical projects, who read the manuscript and made many helpful comments.

MICHAEL KINNAMON
December 1986

CHAPTER I

THE DILEMMA OF THE ECUMENICAL MOVEMENT

Is there an "ecumenical vision" of Christ's church? Or, if not a single vision, are there at least certain basic presuppositions held by most people and churches who have associated themselves with the twentieth-century ecumenical movement? If we can identify several of these presuppositions, can they help us define major issues facing this movement and its participating churches?

A good way to begin discussion of these questions is by responding to two prominent misconceptions about the modern ecumenical movement: that it is not sufficiently concerned with either (1) diversity or (2) truth. Professional ecumenists may object that both charges have been dealt with repeatedly over the past fifty years (as I will indeed show), but my experience with congregations indicates that these misconceptions are far from laid to rest.

DIVERSITY

When I speak with lay groups on ecumenism, for example, it often happens that someone will ask, "Why should I want to worship and think just like all other Christians?" Ecumenical conferences and leaders have never envisioned a unity in which Christians worship, act, and express their faith uniformly. Archbishop Nathan Söderblom, a great ecumenist, spoke of the goal as "unity in multiplicity" at the 1927 Lausanne conference on Faith and Order;[1] and the report of the Faith and Order conference held in 1937 in Edinburgh declared, "What we desire is the unity of a living organism, with the diversity characteristic of the members of a healthy body"[2]—but diversity has become nothing less than an exalted principle of ecumenism

1. See Yves Congar, *Diversity and Communion,* trans. John Bowden (Mystic, Conn.: Twenty-Third Publications, 1985), p. 3.
2. Cited in *A Documentary History of the Faith and Order Movement,* ed. Lukas Vischer (St. Louis: Bethany Press, 1963), p. 63.

since the New Delhi Assembly of the World Council of Churches (WCC) in 1961.[3] That meeting set the tone for subsequent ecumenical reflection with its clear statement that "unity does not imply simple uniformity of organization, rite or expression."[4] One reason for this stronger affirmation was that the diversity of the Christian family was increasingly visible and audible within the WCC itself: four Eastern Orthodox and a number of Third World churches (including eleven from Africa) joined the Council in 1961.

Less than a year after the New Delhi Assembly, Pope John XXIII opened the Second Vatican Council by distinguishing between "the deposit of faith," on which Christians should be agreed, and "the way it is presented," on which they need not agree. That was followed by the *Decree on Ecumenism,* the seminal Vatican II document that echoed a long-standing ecumenical axiom: "While preserving unity in essentials, let everyone in the Church, according to the office entrusted to him, preserve a proper freedom in the various forms of spiritual life and discipline, in the variety of liturgical rites, and even in the theological elaborations of revealed truth. In all things let charity prevail."[5]

The difficulty, of course, comes in determining what is "essential" (an issue to which we will return more than once), but the scope of tolerable diversity seemed definitely to be expanding. In speaking of the disciplines of the Churches of the East (Orthodox), the *Decree* argued that "far from being an obstacle to the Church's unity, such diversity of customs and observances only adds to her comeliness"; and it went on to extend this principle of "legitimate variety" to "differences in theological expressions of doctrine."[6] Subsequent papal statements by both Paul VI and John Paul II have reinforced this conviction.

It was also during the 1960s that the WCC's Faith and Order

---

3. Faith and Order is one of the branches of the ecumenical movement stemming from the Edinburgh World Mission Conference of 1910. In the late 1930s, the Faith and Order Movement (aimed at achieving visible church unity) and the Life and Work Movement (aimed at promoting cooperation among churches on behalf of such issues as peace) joined in order to form what eventually became the World Council of Churches. In 1961 the International Missionary Council became a third major component of the WCC. The specific purposes of Faith and Order continue to be pursued by the WCC's Faith and Order unit.

4. Cited in *A Documentary History of the Faith and Order Movement,* p. 145.

5. *Decree on Ecumenism,* in *Doing the Truth in Charity,* ed. Thomas F. Stransky and John B. Sheerin (New York: Paulist Press, 1982), p. 23.

6. *Decree on Ecumenism,* in *Doing the Truth in Charity,* p. 29.

Commission began to wrestle seriously with the implications for ecumenism of scriptural diversity. An earlier WCC study entitled "Guiding Principles for the Interpretation of the Bible" (1949) had been able to speak without blushing of "the primary message of the Bible,"[7] implying that a common reading of this unique witness to Christ could provide the basis for ecclesiological agreement.

Such optimism was severely shaken, however, at the 1963 Montreal conference on Faith and Order when addresses by biblical scholars Ernst Käsemann and Raymond Brown stressed the diversity of ecclesiologies in the New Testament. Käsemann had already challenged the prevailing ecumenical confidence a decade earlier by contending in an essay that "the New Testament canon does not, as such, constitute the foundation of the unity of the church. On the contrary, . . . it provides the basis for the multiplicity of the confessions."[8] In other words, the Bible, by its internal variety, actually canonizes the diversity of Christianity. At Montreal, Käsemann introduced this perspective directly into the work of Faith and Order when he asserted that "the tensions between Jewish Christian and Gentile Christian churches, between Paul and the Corinthian enthusiasts, between John and early catholicism are as great as those of our own today. . . . To recognize this is even a great comfort and, so far as ecumenical work today is concerned, a theological gain."[9] Why? Because it frees us from a sterile preoccupation with recovering the shape of the New Testament church and opens us to the possibility of a unity that (following Scripture) is richly diverse and oriented toward the future leading of the Spirit.

While Käsemann's paper met with considerable resistance at Montreal, much of his position has since become commonplace in ecumenical discussion. By 1967 the Faith and Order Commission (which was soon to include Roman Catholics) was ready to acknowledge that "awareness of the differences within the Bible will lead us towards a deeper understanding of our divisions and will help us to interpret them more readily as possible and legitimate interpretations of one and the same Gospel." The variety of biblical witness reflects "the diversity of God's actions in different historical situations and the

7. "Guiding Principles for the Interpretation of the Bible," in *The Bible: Its Authority and Interpretation in the Ecumenical Movement,* ed. Ellen Flesseman-Van Leer (Geneva: World Council of Churches, 1980), pp. 13-16.

8. Käsemann, quoted by James D. G. Dunn in *Unity and Diversity in the New Testament: An Inquiry into the Character of Earliest Christianity* (Philadelphia: Westminster Press, 1977), p. 376.

9. Käsemann, *New Testament Questions of Today,* trans. W. J. Montague (Philadelphia: Fortress Press, 1971), pp. 256-57.

diversity of human response to God's actions," and is to be celebrated.[10] The question, they saw, is not how the churches can move
from present diversity into diversity-denying unity (not unity or diversity), but how they can move beyond the limited unities of present
traditions and structures into a unity that encompasses more of the
diverse richness of their common scriptural heritage.

This perspective has clearly helped shape Faith and Order's
widely studied convergence document, *Baptism, Eucharist and Ministry (BEM)*, to which we will turn in Chapter III. It has also found expression in conversations about union such as those in Great Britain
between the United Reformed Church and the Churches of Christ,
which in 1981 led to a union of believers' baptism and infant baptism
traditions. The foundation of our consensus, those churches wrote, is
"the integrity of a mutual recognition of well-grounded convictions."
Those who believe one way on the basis of Scripture and Tradition[11]
need to acknowledge, with regard to baptism, that there are good
grounds in Scripture and Tradition for holding a contrary opinion,
and to accept the integrity of such reconciled disagreement.

Other factors were also challenging previous ecumenical assumptions. At the same time that Käsemann was emphasizing the diversity
of Scripture, delegates to the Montreal conference were exploring the
positive influence of diverse cultural and social contexts on the reading of Scripture and the appropriation of Tradition. There are several
obvious reasons for the emergence of this subject as a major theme
of ecumenical discussion in the 1960s: the reawakening of national
cultures after the era of colonization, an increasing sense of the world
as a "global village," a growing experience in most parts of the world
of the process of secularization and the concomitant pluralism of
philosophies and worldviews, and the influence of the "sociology of
knowledge" school with its insistence that ideas (e.g., theological reflection) cannot be divorced from the social matrix in which they
arise.

It was once possible for ecumenical thinkers such as Arend
van Leeuwen to speak against distinctively regional theologies in
favor of a transcultural ecumenical consensus. Now theologians—
especially those from Asia, Africa, Latin America, and the Pacific—

10. *The Bible: Its Authority and Interpretation in the Ecumenical Movement*, pp. 40, 32.
11. The Montreal conference distinguished between "Tradition" (with a
capital *T*)—"the gospel itself, transmitted from generation to generation in and
by the Church"—and the particular "traditions" through which Tradition has
found expression.

began to reject the idea of a universally valid theology, speaking instead of diverse perspectives on the gospel arising out of differing social, political, and cultural realities (including struggles for liberation). They argued that unity, far from being monolithic, would need to be "intercontextual," culturally diverse.

These insights led to, among other things, a shift in Faith and Order's methodology. Such studies as "Giving Account of the Hope That Is within Us" and "The Community of Women and Men in the Church" took as their starting point the diverse experiences of Christians in local settings. The Indian Roman Catholic scholar Kuncheria Pathil nicely summarizes this inductive, intercontextual approach in his book entitled *Models in Ecumenical Dialogue:*

> The inter-contextual method deals with the question of church unity in the wider context of the tragic divisions in humanity and of the increasing forces of dehumanization in the world on the one hand, and in the context of the growing interdependence in the world and of the general aspiration for the unity of the whole of mankind, on the other. It is a search for unity in diversity, seeking in the diversity of contextual theologies the uniqueness of their particularity as well as their relatedness and their common centre.[12]

The church is both particular and universal. We betray its catholicity, the ecumenical movement affirmed, not by diversity but by conformity and parochialism.

This vision of particularity and universality now shaped the way the WCC thought about its goal of visible church unity (an issue we will explore more fully in Chapter V). The New Delhi Assembly in 1961 suggested that unity be conceived of as the "fully committed fellowship" of "all God's people in each place" (i.e., locally united churches able to share a common life of word and sacrament and to join in common prayer, witness, and service) who are, at the same time, "united with the whole Christian fellowship in all places and all ages."[13] The Nairobi Assembly in 1975 expanded on this statement by speaking of unity as a "conciliar fellowship of local churches which are themselves truly united."[14] This phrase attempted to integrate the

---

12. Pathil, *Models in Ecumenical Dialogue* (Bangalore, India: Dharmaram Publications, 1981), pp. 366-67.

13. *The New Dehli Report,* ed. W. A. Visser 't Hooft (New York: Association Press, 1962), p. 116.

14. *Breaking Barriers: Nairobi 1975,* ed. David Paton (Grand Rapids: Eerdmans, 1976), p. 60.

vision of local eucharistic unity with the demand for a universal fellowship (signified by the ability to meet in an authoritative council) that fully acknowledged the positive character of regional diversity. Roger Mehl captures what I regard as the intention of the Nairobi formula:

> Conciliar unity embraces and welcomes the diversity of traditions and liturgies, the diversity of ecclesiologies (as in the primitive church), the cultural diversity of forms of confessions of faith, the diversity of forms of ministry, the diversity of catechetical methods, and finally, the diversity of sociohistorical forms of church government. . . . The notion of conciliarity obliges us to give up one of the demands often formulated by certain churches, namely that one can only talk of unity when there is total agreement on all possible articles of faith and constitution.[15]

Finally, I want to mention the impact of growing opposition within the ecumenical movement to the evils of racism and, later, sexism. As we will see in Chapter IV, this has led churches in recent years to impose limits on the theological diversity they are willing to accept, but it has also contributed to an appreciation for legitimate human difference. The ecumenical movement has always known that genuine unity rests, as New Delhi put it, on "the reconciling grace which breaks down every wall of race, colour, caste, tribe, sex, class, and nation."[16] But instead of leading to the idea that "everyone is pretty much the same" (a phrase I sometimes hear in well-meaning American congregations), this affirmation of oneness in Christ has led ecumenical churches to celebrate the distinctive colors and cultures that make up Christian community. Theologians such as Jürgen Moltmann began to argue that the church should not be seeking uniformity but should be working through the ecumenical movement to expand its range of unlikeness. The church "breaks through the law of human society according to which like only draws to like. It is made up of Jews and Gentiles, masters and servants, the educated and the uneducated, men and women, and this is the only way in which it proves that the spirit of Christ lives in it."[17] When Paul speaks of the power of Christian fellowship, observed Moltmann, the

---

15. Mehl, quoted by Congar in *Diversity and Communion*, p. 4.

16. Cited in *A Documentary History of the Faith and Order Movement*, p. 148.

17. Moltmann, "Hope and Development," in *The Future of Creation: Collected Essays*, trans. Margaret Kohl (Philadelphia: Fortress Press, 1979), p. 54.

Greek word he uses is not *philia,* love of that which is beautiful and similar, but *agape,* creative love of that which is different, alien, ugly. The church dare not be a community of like individuals who affirm each other; rather, it must be a community of unlike individuals who know themselves to be affirmed together by the grace of God.

Many ecumenists might not go quite so far, but the trend toward wider acceptance of diversity seems undeniable. Along with the question "How can we build the consensus needed for unity?" one hears the question "How can we build sufficient trust to live with more difference?"

TRUTH

All of this emphasis on diversity, however, has led to other problems. "Of course you can afford to be ecumenical," I was once told by a caller on a radio talk show, "because you don't take the truth of Christ very seriously!" Even among its supporters, ecumenism is sometimes thought of as a matter of democratic toleration. ("Toleration," wrote Chesterton, "is the virtue of people who do not believe anything.") Or it is viewed as a necessary accommodation to the pluralism of the age. It is apparently assumed that churches not involved in ecumenical dialogue are characterized by a tenacious hold on truth, while ecumenical churches are willing to waffle for the sake of fellowship. "The problem," says church historian Martin Marty, "is that the civil people are not committed and the committed people aren't civil"[18]—or at least that is the suspicion.

The issue at stake is more precisely stated by the British evangelical A. T. Houghton. He writes, "An impression has been given that unity is of such importance that it can be treated as an isolated concept, and the pursuit of unity can be regarded as a goal to be reached regardless of the principles involved."[19] Although I will contend that this is essentially a misconception, the ecumenical movement has undoubtedly been guilty at times of glossing over major differences between truth claims. Lukas Vischer, former director of the Faith and Order Commission, has observed that theological agreements produced during the early years of the movement often "rest upon carefully thought-out formulations which, although able to be accepted in one way or another by all those present, nevertheless

18. Marty, quoted by Robert Jewett in *Christian Tolerance: Paul's Message to the Modern Church* (Philadelphia: Westminster Press, 1982), p. 9.
19. Houghton, "Unity, Truth and Mission," in *Evangelicals and Unity,* ed. J. D. Douglas (Appleford, England: Marcham Manor Press, 1964), p. 32.

have different meanings for different people."[20] Faith and Order's early method was commonly known as "comparative ecclesiology" (the various traditions shared their doctrinal positions in order to discover whether each could recognize in others certain elements of the church), and it did tend to avoid hard debate on conflicting understandings of truth.

It was at the Lund conference on Faith and Order in 1952 that a new methodology, often called the "Christological method," was first articulated. The Lutheran theologian Edmund Schlink has referred to the methodology as a Copernican revolution in ecumenism: instead of seeing the other ecclesial bodies as planets rotating around "us" and "our" center of truth, the churches were now encouraged to see Christ as the sun around whom all revolve.[21] Faith and Order now affirmed that we grow closer to one another by growing closer to Christ, who is the center of the Christian circle. The idea is not so much "to protect" truth as to discover its fullness through ecumenical readings of Scripture, Tradition, and God's action in the contemporary world. The Catholic theologian Hans Küng wrote, "A Church which truly desires to find unity with other Churches must be a lover and follower of truth, completely devoted to truth, it must be a Church which knows in all humility that it is not the manifestation of the whole truth, that it has not fulfilled the whole truth, a Church which knows that it must be led anew by the spirit of truth into all truth."[22] We will explore the theological basis for such a conviction in the next chapter, but for now it is enough to acknowledge that it articulates a perspective commonly expressed in ecumenical discussion, especially since the Lund conference.

Actually, the World Council has always proclaimed its commitment to unity in truth. The Council's first assembly, held in Amsterdam in 1948, likely had John 17 in mind when it wrote that "there is no gain in unity unless it is unity in truth and holiness."[23] Two years later the famous Toronto Statement on the nature of the WCC addressed the issue even more directly:

> There are critics, and not infrequently friends, of the ecumenical movement who criticize or praise it for its alleged in-

20. Vischer, cited in *A Documentary History of the Faith and Order Movement*, pp. 9-10.
21. See Schlink, "The Unity and Diversity of the Church," in *What Unity Implies* (Geneva: World Council of Churches, 1969).
22. Küng, *The Church* (Garden City, N.Y.: Image Books, 1976), p. 376.
23. Cited in *A Documentary History of the Faith and Order Movement*, p. 81.

herent latitudinarianism. According to them the ecumenical movement stands for the fundamental equality of all Christian doctrines and conceptions of the Church and is, therefore, not concerned with the question of truth. This misunderstanding is due to the fact that ecumenism has in the minds of these persons become identified with certain particular theories about unity, which have indeed played a role in ecumenical history, but which do not represent the common view of the movement as a whole, and have never been officially endorsed by the World Council.[24]

The New Delhi Assembly, which so emphasized diversity, also lifted up the pursuit of truth in a way that echoes the Lund conference: "We cannot and must not surrender those truths and ways of church life which we believe are God's will for his Church, and which the others do not yet accept. At the same time, we cannot and should not refuse to move out to Christ whose presence we recognize in the life of the others."[25] And Vatican II's *Decree on Ecumenism* certainly reinforced the point. "Nothing," it argues, "is so foreign to the spirit of ecumenism as a false irenicism" that seeks compromise of theological positions rather than the fullness of truth through honest sharing of disagreement.[26] This warning has been repeated countless times by Protestants and Catholics alike. "There is all the distance in the world," writes theologian John Macquarrie, "between a comprehensiveness that has seriously faced differences and sought to embrace the very truth expressed in the difference itself, and a vacuousness which, by accepting every point of view, denies any truth claim to all of them."[27] The intent of serious ecumenism is most definitely the former.

To my mind, a classic statement of this concern for truth is found in a 1966 article by the WCC's first general secretary, Willem Visser 't Hooft, the towering figure of twentieth-century ecumenism. He declared that if the new interest in pluralism leads to a relativism in which one answer to the ultimate questions of life is as good as the next, then we should oppose it as an invention of the devil. Genuine ecumenical dialogue must be understood as "spiritual battle for truth,"

24. Cited in *A Documentary History of the Faith and Order Movement,* p. 170.
25. Cited in *A Documentary History of the Faith and Order Movement,* p. 154.
26. *Decree on Ecumenism,* in *Doing the Truth in Charity,* p. 26.
27. Macquarrie, *Christian Unity and Christian Diversity* (Philadelphia: Westminster Press, 1975), p. 47.

although, he added, it is a common battle against error and not a fight between partners based on the assumption that one is already right and one wrong[28] (a point to which we will return in Chapter II). At their best, ecumenical Christians should be so committed to living the whole truth of the Christian faith that they readily confess that this truth is far greater than any of their separated witnesses.

The willingness of ecumenical bodies to make unambiguous statements about God's will for the church, even when these statements are or may be divisive, has actually grown stronger during the past decade (perhaps indicating an increase in trust among participating churches). *Baptism, Eucharist and Ministry,* for example, while accused of compromise on some issues, uses Scripture and Tradition to challenge widespread understandings of the eucharist that would reduce it to individualistic acts of pious recollection. At one point it declares that "all kinds of injustice, racism, separation and lack of freedom are radically challenged when we share in the body and blood of Christ"[29]—hardly the language of easy compromise! Meanwhile, WCC assemblies have definitely not refrained from speaking forcefully about what they perceive to be the truth of Christian discipleship. The delegates at the Vancouver Assembly in 1983 expressed their conviction "that apartheid stands condemned by the Gospel of Jesus Christ, the life of the world, and that any theology which supports or condones it is heretical," and spoke of opposition to "the production, deployment and use of nuclear weapons" not as one option for Christians but as a matter of "faithfulness to the Gospel."[30]

COMMUNITY

A strong endorsement of diversity can lead to at least one other result consistently rejected by the ecumenical movement: individualism. People are simply different, the argument runs. Some like Coca-Cola; others prefer Pepsi. Some like the Methodist Church; others prefer the Catholic. It is all up to the individual. Just give him or her the room to respond to God in his or her own way.

By contrast, the ecumenical movement has insisted that diverse

28. See Visser 't Hooft, "Pluralism—Temptation or Opportunity?" *Ecumenical Review,* Apr. 1966, p. 147.

29. *Baptism, Eucharist and Ministry* (Geneva: World Council of Churches, 1983), par. E20.

30. *Gathered for Life: Official Report, VI Assembly of the World Council of Churches,* ed. David Gill (Geneva: World Council of Churches, 1983), pp. 154-55, 137.

individuals committed to truth need each other, that *community* is the context within which various claims are continually tested and enriched. Parker Palmer, a well-known writer on spirituality and education, notes,

> Too many of us subscribe to a weak doctrine of pluralism, to the simple notion that truth looks different when viewed from different angles. Because this notion concedes diversity without calling us into dialogue, it leaves us in isolation and destroys community as effectively as the objectivism it seeks to resist. Eventually, this theory of relativity leads to a war of all against all where power, not truth, prevails.[31]

The Methodist ecumenist J. Robert Nelson puts the point more poetically. The church, he argues, must resist a secular notion of pluralism "where rats race, dogs eat dogs, and the sting of affluent WASPs can paralyze most others in their economic and political tracks."[32] Christian diversity must not serve as a cover for a rugged individualism in which each looks out for himself or herself, even at the expense of others. The world speaks of toleration for the sake of civil harmony among free individuals; the church speaks of *koinonia* (fellowship, mutual participation) as a manifestation of our love for God and neighbor. The diverse parts of Christ's body dare not say to each other "I have no need of you" or "Your plight is of no concern to me."

Perhaps the biggest contribution of the ecumenical movement to Christian life in this century has been its dogged conviction that the church matters, that the community of the faithful is of central significance to our relationship with God. That may sound funny to some contemporary ears. But it should be remembered that over the past two hundred years, Protestants (especially in America) have emphasized the private, experiential dimension of Christianity. Religion seemed squeezed out of public life by the dominance of the scientific worldview, becoming a matter of individual quests for meaning determined by personal preference. What the ecumenical movement has tried to stress, in line with the biblical tradition, is that God is not simply pursued in isolation but is responded to and known within the realm of covenant relations, within the community of others who have heard God's Word and responded—in various ways.

31. Palmer, *To Know As We Are Known: A Spirituality of Education* (San Francisco: Harper & Row, 1983), p. 66.

32. Nelson, "The Inclusive Church," *Christian Century,* 20 Feb. 1985, p. 184.

There is a curious irony in this shift. The Enlightenment thinkers feared community and endorsed individualistic religion in order to protect the tolerance of diversity; when religion became communal, it seemed to become intolerant, insisting that all conform to prescribed norms. Today ecumenical Christians see the dangers of individualism and the need for community, and they are convinced that community can promote "tolerance" by insisting that we need each other. Thus the WCC's first assembly proclaimed that "it is our common concern for [the] Church which draws us together."[33] And it is this concern which continues to unite the WCC's three priority concerns (inherited from the organizations that preceded it): promoting visible church unity (Faith and Order), addressing together the wider context of human brokenness (Life and Work), and proclaiming together the Word of God (International Missionary Council). Indeed, if asked to boil ecumenism down to a single, unifying question, I would answer: What does it mean to be the church, the whole Christian community, living in obedience to the will of God?

THE LIMITS OF ACCEPTABLE DIVERSITY

The preceding pages point toward the main theme of this book: namely, that the vision behind the ecumenical movement is best understood as a constant and necessary tension between truth and diverse community. Christians are called and empowered to be a diverse community of mutually supporting love *and* to bear witness, through proclamation and discipleship, to the truth of God, especially as that is revealed in Jesus Christ. The question of the unity we seek comes down to the way we relate these two "givens" of our common life. Churches will undoubtedly conceive of this relationship in quite different ways. Some will stress that truth is the basis for real community, others that community is the context for discovering truth. But the tension is inescapable.

This affirmation of both diversity and truth also poses what I take to be the central issue facing the contemporary ecumenical movement: How do we determine the limits of acceptable diversity? The eminent Roman Catholic ecumenist Yves Congar expressed it this way in a 1980 article: "I think the prime theological problem raised by ecumenism today is that of specifying as far as possible what differences are compatible with the establishment of full communion.

---

33. Cited in *A Documentary History of the Faith and Order Movement*, p. 76.

What diversity can authentic organic unity admit?"[34] And, beyond that, what methodology do we have for answering such a question?

The church has, of course, lived with these dilemmas for nearly two thousand years. The First Epistle of John is the clearest instance in the New Testament of a diversity becoming so unacceptable that it necessitated separation. In this century, the struggle during the 1930s between the Confessing Church and the German Christian Movement left an indelible mark on ecumenism (since many early ecumenical leaders, including Dietrich Bonhoeffer, were directly involved in the struggle). This imprint can be felt in the following warning from Edmund Schlink: "The most important and decisive reason for the various limitations of the diversity possible within unity is the concern to maintain the distinction between truth and error, between the Church and the pseudo-church, i.e., the concern about the danger of apostasy."[35]

It is my judgment that this issue has become particularly acute again in this decade. Several examples come quickly to mind.

First, questions of "heresy" have been raised explicitly in recent years around the evil of apartheid. The World Alliance of Reformed Churches (WARC) at its 1982 meeting in Ottawa declared that the South African situation constitutes "a *status confessionis* for our Churches, which means that we regard this as an issue on which it is not possible to differ without seriously jeopardizing the integrity of our common confession as Reformed Churches."[36] In other words, the theological justification of apartheid is an unacceptable diversity, a denial of Christian truth, over which it may be necessary to break fellowship. The WARC consequently suspended the membership of two Afrikaner churches. The Lutheran World Federation (LWF) did the same at its 1984 assembly in Budapest.

Second, there is a growing frustration among ecumenically oriented theologians who claim that just when the ecumenical movement seems to be making theological progress (e.g., *Baptism, Eucharist and Ministry*), this work is undercut either by church hierarchies that appear to insist on ever greater levels of agreement (i.e., less diversity) or by social activists who dismiss or minimize doctrinal reconciliation in favor of nearly nonnegotiable commitments on social issues.

34. Congar, "Trials and Promises of Ecumenism," in *Voices of Unity*, ed. Ans J. van der Bent (Geneva: World Council of Churches, 1981), p. 31.

35. Schlink, "The Unity and Diversity of the Church," p. 34.

36. Cited in *Apartheid Is a Heresy*, ed. John W. de Gruchy and Charles Villa-Vicencio (Grand Rapids: Eerdmans, 1983), p. 170.

Third, the polarization of "ecumenical" and "evangelical" Christians seems still to be increasing (despite some hopeful signs), fed by stereotypes and half-truths that revolve around the question of truth and diversity. "By 1970," writes Martin Marty in *The Public Church,* "a new law of history was developing. If you wish to evangelize, you must be cocksure, absolutist, unfriendly to other Christians. . . . To be ecumenical meant to be half-believers, certainly nonevangelizers."[37] Such a summary is obviously unfair to both sides, but it points to the widespread tendency of ecumenists to dismiss evangelicalism as interested only in its version of truth at the expense of unity, and the widespread tendency of evangelicals to dismiss ecumenism as interested only in its vision of unity at the expense of truth.

Of course, evangelicals are not the only ones who are often accused of being excessively preoccupied with uniform truth claims. A fourth example of the resurgence of the unity-within-diversity issue is the Vatican's recent charges of serious doctrinal errors against Brazilian theologian Leonardo Boff and American ethicist Charles Curran, which have certainly sparked debate on the limits of tolerable diversity in the Roman Catholic Church. Such controversy has also been fueled by the book entitled *Unity of the Churches: An Actual Possibility,* written by the distinguished theologians Heinrich Fries and Karl Rahner. Joseph Cardinal Ratzinger, prefect of Rome's Congregation for the Doctrine of the Faith, has contended that the book promotes a false unity by skipping over the truth issue with "a couple of ecclesiastico-political maneuvers."

Fifth, the scandal of Jim Jones—ordained and uncensured by my denomination, the Christian Church (Disciples of Christ)—has been a vivid reminder to American Protestants that not all things done in the name of Christ are Christian. Perhaps an even more insidious example is "identity theology," a so-called Christian theological movement used to justify white racist ideologies in parts of the United States. I feel confident that most Christians would view this movement as a "pseudo-church" not deserving of inclusion in the wider fellowship of the followers of Christ.

Sixth, following the Vancouver Assembly in 1983, a study was initiated by the WCC to examine the occasional incoherence of diverse theologies in its programs. J. Robert Nelson sees the problem this way:

No one, presumably, would want or expect the formation of

---

37. Marty, *The Public Church: Mainline-Evangelical-Catholic* (New York: Crossroad, 1981), p. 71.

one official theological position to inform all policies. But are there limits to diversity within the terms of the Council's constitution? Is it possible to determine when certain theological views within the Council structure are mutually exclusive, and thus incoherent, rather than differing modes of expression of the same Christian faith?[38]

THE LIMITS OF ACCEPTABLE UNITY

Perhaps it will clarify matters to make the same point from the opposite direction, starting not with diversity but with unity. No idea is more central to the ecumenical movement than the concept that the church is "essentially, intentionally and constitutionally" one.[39] A divided church, as Scripture understands it, is simply a contradiction in terms. Through baptism an individual no longer has an independent existence but becomes part of a local community that is itself a member of one body (1 Cor. 12), a branch of a single vine (John 15), one stone among many composing the house of faith (1 Pet. 2). The Gospel of John presents Jesus as praying that his followers may experience the unity he has with the Father (17:21). The Letter to the Ephesians makes unity its primary theme, reminding us that "there is one body and one Spirit, just as you were called to the one hope that belongs to your call, one Lord, one faith, one baptism, one God and Father of us all, who is above all and through all and in all" (4:4-6). Paul's letter to the church in Rome represents a mighty attempt to show that God is served not by the victory of the Hellenizers over the Judaizers, or vice versa, but by their willingness to live together, with differences, in community on the basis of their common experience of grace though faith in Christ Jesus (Rom. 14). Therefore, Paul exclaims, "welcome one another . . . as Christ has welcomed you, for the glory of God" (Rom. 15:7).

There is little doubt that disunity makes the work of Christian service more difficult. It also undermines witness and evangelism, especially in places like Asia, where the church is a small minority yet still splintered into competing groups. But most ecumenists insist, in light of Scripture, that unity is not pursued for purely functional reasons, that disunity is not just an inconvenient obstacle to a better use of Christian resources. It is disobedience to God's will that we be one, a

38. Nelson, "Beyond Vancouver: A Vital and Coherent World Council of Churches," *Ecumenical Trends*, Oct. 1984, p. 131.

39. The phrase is from Thomas Campbell's "Declaration and Address" (1809), the foundational document of the Disciples of Christ.

denial of the unity that is given us in Christ. Cardinal Ratzinger (in the eyes of many, an unlikely source on this topic) captures this perspective when he writes that "we must learn that unity is a Christian truth pertaining to the very essence of Christianity. . . . [The churches] should not be forever asking if union or recognition of the other is justifiable, but rather if continued separation is justifiable; not union but division requires defense."[40]

This brings us back, however, to our main argument. Unity may be at the heart of the gospel, but, as we have seen, the ecumenical vision affirms not simply the truth of unity but unity in truth. Cardinal Ratzinger's assertion is surely right, but so is the following observation of Gregory Baum, a Catholic theologian widely known for his commitment to ecumenism:

> Visible unity of Christians is not an end unless it includes unity with the Lord Jesus. One could easily imagine Christians of a certain country all belonging to a single Church and yet being without much faith, lacking in hope, and not deeply moved by divine charity. In such a situation, the division of Christians, if understood as a sign of God and a source of renewal, could even be a blessing.[41]

Visser 't Hooft highlights another dimension of this issue when he points to a fundamental tension between unity and renewal in the history of the church. "There have been those," he observes, "for whom the Church has no meaning unless it exemplifies the life of the new creation in constant renewal of life; there have been those to whom the Church as given in history is so precious that they look with suspicion upon any outbreak of new life which might affect the unity and peace of the Church."[42] The distinctive genius of the modern ecumenical movement is to insist that unity and renewal are inseparable, which is another way of saying that there are limits to acceptable unity. We will explore those limits throughout this book, but one marker emerges from the argument of this chapter: Unity that is not inclusive of human diversity—racial, cultural, theological, liturgical diversity—is not the unity God wills. The ecumenical movement has wagered that unity is possible apart from authoritarian, uniformity-

40. Ratzinger, "The Future of Ecumenism," *Theology Digest,* Fall 1987, p. 203.
41. Baum, "Drawing Closer Together," in *Steps to Christian Unity,* ed. John A. O'Brien (Garden City, N.Y.: Doubleday, 1964), p. 278.
42. Visser 't Hooft, *The Renewal of the Church* (London: SCM Press, 1956), p. 117.

producing structures—indeed, that this is what God is calling us to make manifest.

As I read it, however, a rather subtle shift has taken place in ecumenical thinking on just this score. A quotation from the WCC's Evanston Assembly in 1954 may help exemplify what I have in mind: "There is a diversity which is not sinful but good because it reflects both the diversities of the gifts of the Spirit in the one body and diversities of creation by the one Creator. But when diversity disrupts the manifest unity of the body, then it changes character and becomes sinful division."[43] Leading figures in the current movement would agree, but I suspect that many would add a large caveat: While we must work to overcome sinful divisions, often inherited from the past, *new* divisions may be necessary—or, better, inevitable—because they reflect the rejection of untruth in our era. The issue again is the nature of genuine unity. German theologian Dorothea Soelle reminds us that the Roman Empire was united, but its "peace," the *Pax Romana,* was based on coercive domination of the impoverished. The *Pax Christi,* the new unity and peace promised and made possible in Christ, was good news precisely for those who suffered under the *Pax Romana.* This insight, brought home by the injustice of our day, has meant a greater willingness by those committed to seeking unity to acknowledge its limits.

The most forceful statement of this perspective may be that of the Latin American Protestant theologian José Miguez Bonino, a former president of the WCC. According to him, the ideal of "pluralism," the notion of a "'complex unity' which embraces many and sometimes seemingly contradictory options," is only partially true, and may actually become an instrument of domination that hides the real nature of the conflicts between contemporary Christians. Specifically, these have to do with "questions of dependence and domination, of racial oppression, of poverty and economic justice, of human and social rights," which are by no means peripheral issues in the life of the church. This leads Miguez Bonino to suggest his own limits: "The test of the unity of the Church can only be, therefore, its interpretative and praxical ability to overcome—in reality and not only in the realm of ideas—the concrete unfreedoms and destructive conflicts of our present history in the direction of the kingdom."[44]

43. Cited in *A Documentary History of the Faith and Order Movement,* p. 136.

44. Miguez Bonino, "A Latin American Attempt to Locate the Question of Unity," in *What Kind of Unity?* (Geneva: World Council of Churches, 1974), pp. 51-62.

Glenn Tinder makes a similar argument in his book *Tolerance: Toward a New Civility* by distinguishing between "unity" and "community." The former can be created by force and deceit, while the latter "denotes a relationship in which persons are freely and fully present to one another." "Through terror and propaganda, dictators ostensibly seeking total *community* have created societies of such total *unity* that community was impossible; hence the paradox of tyrannies: monolithic unity joined with radical alienation."[45]

Throughout this book I use both "unity" and "community" as positive terms, but by doing so I am actually indicating my fundamental agreement with Tinder's point: a unity that does not exhibit the values of diverse, liberating, truth-seeking community is not the unity we seek. Unity and diversity have their limits. In the remainder of this book, we will examine how the ecumenical movement has determined what these limits are, and my view of how these limits should be determined.

45. Tinder, *Tolerance: Toward a New Civility* (Amherst: University of Massachusetts Press, 1976), p. 153.

CHAPTER II

FOUNDATIONS FOR THE ECUMENICAL VISION

The first chapter was largely descriptive, showing that truth, diversity, and genuine community are crucial concepts for the ecumenical movement's emerging vision of the church. In this chapter I want to move beyond description to identify five theological assumptions, or sets of assumptions, on which this vision rests. There is not—cannot be—a single "theology of ecumenism," but it is fair to say that most of the observations I will make in this chapter have been repeatedly endorsed, though perhaps in quite different language, in ecumenical discussion. They have to do generally with (1) the sovereign love of God, (2) the saving grace of Jesus Christ, (3) the revelation of God's Word, especially through Scripture, (4) the nature of truth, and (5) the church as a community of dialogue. In the last section of the chapter, I will come at all of this from a different angle by arguing that ecumenism is fundamentally concerned with the problem of idolatry.

FIVE THEOLOGICAL AFFIRMATIONS

1. The ecumenical vision rests ultimately on the sovereignty of God, which relativizes *all* human concepts, institutions, and activities. Human claims to truth stand under judgment of the One who alone is holy, the One who transcends all of our projects and explanations—a realization to which Scripture testifies on practically every page.

> To whom will you liken me and make me equal, and compare me, that we may be alike? . . . I am God, and there is no other; I am God, and there is none like me. (Isa. 46:5, 9)

> For my thoughts are not your thoughts, neither are your ways my ways, says the Lord. For as the heavens are higher than the earth, so are my ways higher than your ways and my thoughts than your thoughts. (Isa. 55:8-9)

> The God who made the world and everything in it, being
> Lord of heaven and earth, does not live in shrines made by
> man, nor is he served by human hands, as though he needed
> anything, since he himself gives to all men life and breath and
> everything. . . . "In him we live and move and have our
> being." (Acts 17:24-25, 28)

The American theologian Gordon Kaufman surely has history on
his side when he claims that the idea of such a God is a most dangerous thing. Mortals constantly seek to domesticate the transcendent,
visualizing God as a private patron who offers absolute sanction for
their version of the status quo. But, says Kaufman, a scriptural understanding of God should lead us to precisely opposite conclusions: "If
God is not converted into an idol sustaining and supporting our own
projects, but is apprehended as truly *God,* the judge of all the earth,
the self is forced into a posture of humbleness in its claims, and a
principle of revolutionary criticism of all the structures and orders of
the human becomes effectual."[1] We know our finitude in relation to
the One who is infinite. We know that we are not the source and
measure of truth in relation to the One who, we confess, is the
source and measure of all things. The insights claimed by the "sociology of knowledge" that all thought and valuation are existentially
bound—and cannot, therefore, be regarded as absolutely or universally true or valid—are actually corollaries of the theological doctrine
of divine sovereignty and human finitude.

The real point I want to stress, however, is that such "theological
relativity" is impossible without a faith in the existence of ultimate
truth. There may be no better statement of this than the first two
commandments from Sinai. The first commandment ("You shall have
no other gods before me") calls us to see that our commitment of
faith must be to the one God of Israel whom Jesus called "Abba," the
Truth above all truths; but the second ("You shall not make for yourself a graven image") immediately reminds us that our grasp of that
Truth is never final.[2] In Scripture idolatry is frequently associated with
visual objects, but the Christian tradition has long recognized that
idolatry takes more subtle forms. As John Wesley wrote, "We have
set up idols in our hearts; . . . we worship ourselves when we pay

---

1. Kaufman, *The Theological Imagination: Constructing the Concept of
God* (Philadelphia: Westminster Press, 1981), p. 87. Chapter III of this book has
informed my whole discussion of the link between the sovereignty of God and
the idea of relativity.
2. See Robert Jewett, *Christian Tolerance: Paul's Message to the Modern
Church* (Philadelphia: Westminster Press, 1982), pp. 68-73.

that honor to ourselves which is due to God alone; therefore all pride is idolatry." Our own era has come to see, perhaps more clearly than our ancestors, that there are indeed such things as "graven image theologies" which idolatrously claim to present full verbal pictures of that which is transcendent. "There is a principled basis for intellectual humility in the second commandment," writes biblical scholar Robert Jewett in his book *Christian Tolerance,* "one that opens the human community to an ongoing quest for adequate, though never final, formulations of the truth. If one had the Second Commandment without the First, however, the severity of such an aniconic faith would quickly drift into despair and nihilism."[3] Those who claim that there is absolute truth are right, as are those who maintain the relativity all human truth claims. These are opposite sides of the same doctrinal coin. The point is that we are God's, not that God is ours. Our task is to conform to God's will, not to insist that everyone else conform to ours. Or, as Jürgen Moltmann puts it, "It is not our claim on the truth which is absolute, but the claim of the truth on us."[4]

2. The second observation is more difficult to formulate precisely because it is actually a cluster of affirmations having to do with the grace of God, especially as that is revealed in Jesus Christ. The foundation of all Christian identity is the biblical confession of Jesus as Christ and Lord (Matt. 16:16). While we may share common hopes and expressions of love with those of other faiths, we are distinguished as Christians by our belief that "in Christ God was reconciling the world to himself" (2 Cor. 5:19). All confessional differences, ecumenists have generally affirmed, are secondary to the unity we share as a result of our common experience of grace through faith in Jesus Christ. Our baptism into Christ binds us as members of one family of faith whose shared experience of the gracious love of God, a love beyond any possible deserving, is stronger than any dissimilarities among us. This point was forcefully made in Vatican II's *Decree on Ecumenism,* as Pope John Paul II reminded the Roman Curia in a 1985 address:

> One of the salient aspects of Christian truth, which the Second Vatican Council brought fully to light, is the profound communion—even though still imperfect—already existing among all those who have been justified through faith in Jesus Christ, who are incorporated in him through baptism

---

3. Jewett, *Christian Tolerance,* p. 72.
4. Moltmann, "What Kind of Unity?" in *Lausanne 77* (Geneva: World Council of Churches, 1977), p. 45.

and are enlivened by the Holy Spirit. Therefore we rightly recognize them as brothers in the Lord.[5]

I have heard William Lazareth, former director of the WCC's Faith and Order Commission, contend that the object of the ecumenical movement is to improve our grammar. Confessional labels, even if preserved in future models of unity (a debate we will pursue in Chapter V), can be no more than adjectives signifying particular perspectives and traditions in the one body of Christ; "Christian" is the noun that indicates our basic identity—and Christ is not divided.

There are numerous implications of this Christological foundation that are important for ecumenism. I want to mention two of them briefly.

First, the one thing Paul clearly would not compromise in his struggles with the Roman, Corinthian, and Galatian churches was the conviction that we are justified not by works of the Law nor by the correctness of our doctrine but by grace through faith in the crucified and risen Lord. This unmerited gift should serve as a further reminder that neither we nor our churches possess the fullness of truth but are given love as a basis of community because we need each other. Beyond that, the free gift of grace that we gratefully acknowledge in our lives should open us to the likelihood—to the hope—that this gift has also been given to others who confess faith in Christ, though often in language different from our own. "The ultimate basis for ecumenical theology," writes Karl Rahner, whose experience with the subject is extensive, "is the unity, apprehended in hope, of a belief in justifying grace which already exists and is identical on both sides"—but which our theologies have not yet commonly expressed. In other words, ecumenical Christians are convinced that their partners in dialogue through faith live already in the grace of God. Churches in ecumenical dialogue are not seeking to create a unity of faith in one another but, in Rahner's words, "are mutually crediting one another with already having it" and are, therefore, exploring together ways of understanding, living, and expressing it ever more truly.[6]

Second, a focus on Christ could lead—and has, at times, led—to a vision of the church as the triumphant sign of Christ's risen body. Without denying this, the tendency today is to emphasize far more the one servant community at the foot of the cross. Moltmann perhaps expresses this best:

5. Cited in *Origins,* 18 July 1975, p. 127.
6. Rahner, *Theological Investigations,* vol. 14, trans. David Bourke (New York: Seabury Press, 1976), pp. 248-49.

> The unity of the church can only be a unity in truth, and the
> truth which demands unity and makes it possible is the all-
> embracing and all-saving truth of his sacrificial death on the
> cross at Golgotha. . . . Ecumenism comes into being
> wherever—and this is everywhere—we find ourselves under
> the cross of Christ and there recognize each other as
> brothers and sisters who are hungry in the same poverty (Ro-
> mans 3:23) and imprisoned in the selfsame sin. Under the
> cross we all stand empty-handed.[7]

The cross convicts us of all pride, all pretensions to absolute truth and
goodness. Just as the poor are blessed by not being tied to the things
of this world, so those who stand empty-handed under the cross
should not be tied to the things that give us worldly identity.

3. One possible rejoinder to the first two principles is that the ultimate truth of God's will as revealed in Christ is *directly* accessible to
human beings, especially through the witness of Scripture. It is this
assumption that has been thoroughly undermined in the twentieth
century. Even if we hold that every word of Scripture is divinely inspired or that the Holy Spirit guides us through events in our daily
lives, we still must acknowledge that we see—interpret—these words
and acts of guidance through glasses formed by cultural, historical,
and confessional (i.e., finite) perspectives. As one recent WCC study
puts it, "A fully objective interpretation of scripture is impossible because no interpreter, or community of interpreters, can be divorced
from the prejudices that accompany his/her immersion in time. . . .
Our experience constitutes a vital partner in the unending dialogue
with God's Living Word."[8]

There are at least two sources of this emphasis on the inevitability
and positive significance of interpretation.

First, research in virtually every scholarly discipline has reinforced
the point, referred to in Chapter I, that the way people see the world
or understand a text is dramatically shaped by the language they use,
the culture in which they participate, and the history through which
they live. Indeed, in *The Meaning of Revelation,* H. Richard Niebuhr
goes so far as to contend that

> no other influence has affected twentieth century thought

---

7. Moltmann, *The Passion for Life: A Messianic Lifestyle,* trans. M. Douglas Meeks (Philadelphia: Fortress Press, 1978), pp. 82, 84.

8. "The Authority of Scripture in Light of the New Experiences of Women,"
in *In God's Image,* ed. Janet Crawford and Michael Kinnamon (Geneva: World
Council of Churches, 1983), p. 57.

more deeply than the discovery of spatial and temporal relativity. The understanding that the spatio-temporal point of
view of an observer entered into his knowledge of reality, so
that no universal knowledge of things as they are in themselves is possible, so that all knowledge is conditioned by the
standpoint of the knower, plays the same role in our thinking
that the idealistic discoveries of the seventeenth and eigh-
teenth centuries and the evolutionary discovery of the
nineteenth played in the thought of earlier generations.[9]

Second, this new insight into the relativity of human perspectives
(an insight, as I argued previously, that can also be derived from an
affirmation of God's sovereignty and transcendence) has helped biblical scholars see that Scripture itself reveals a process of interpretation. A four-year Faith and Order study (1968-1971) entitled "The
Authority of the Bible" concludes that "the events which the Bible
claims to be decisively important have already in every case been subject to interpretation." Every reconstruction of "what really happened" can be only a hypothesis offered in faith. "The events re-
ported are therefore never the 'bare facts,' but are always accessible
to us only in the clothing of their interpretation by the biblical
authors."[10]

Commenting on the Faith and Order study, Hans-Ruedi Weber,
the well-known biblical scholar and WCC staff member, argues that
what is canonical for Christians is not only the content of the Bible but
also the interpretive process that we see in it.[11] What Scripture shows
is a community attempting to interpret the continuing presence of the
living God in terms of its inherited tradition. "The present generation," says the Faith and Order report, "enters into the process of interpretation in which the witnesses of that past time were also en-
gaged. On the basis of the interpretation they have bequeathed to us,
we must try to catch a glimpse of the facts which they were interpret-
ing and to do in our situation what they did in theirs."[12]

All of this, along with the new awareness of the diversity within

9. Niebuhr, The Meaning of Revelation (New York: Macmillan, 1960),
p. 5.
10. "The Authority of the Bible," in The Bible: Its Authority and Interpretation in the Ecumenical Movement, ed. Ellen Flesseman-Van Leer
(Geneva: World Council of Churches, 1980), p. 48.
11. Weber, Experiments with Bible Study (Geneva: World Council of
Churches, 1981), p. 51.
12. "The Authority of the Bible," in The Bible: Its Authority and Interpretation in the Ecumenical Movement, p. 51.

Scripture talked about in Chapter I, has had powerful ecumenical consequences. It is harder to claim that one's confession has an absolute hold on truth when it is viewed as a historically conditioned interpretation of the Bible's own effort to read the signs of God's redemptive activity. As Raymond Brown puts it, "Both ecumenics and biblical studies should make us aware that there are other ways of being faithful to which we do not do justice."[13] And we need not deny that our own way is faithful in order to make such a statement.

It is obvious, however, that some churches reject such a conclusion, arguing that it leads to relativism (not just relativity of human perspective) and skepticism—that is, the idea that "one opinion is as good as another because real knowledge of truth is impossible." If the ecumenical movement is really interested in truth, doesn't it have to agree that some interpretations of Scripture are better—truer—than others?

Are there principles for helping achieve "truer interpretation"? At least two have emerged from ecumenical discussion (and the scholarly community) that I find compelling.

First, and most important, the movement has insisted that interpretation must be undertaken by the whole church, that the community of interpreters must be expanded if we are serious about articulating for this generation more of the truth of the gospel. Earlier in this century the ecumenical movement stressed that the community of interpreters must be *confessionally* expanded: Anglicans need Presbyterians, and vice versa, in their attempt to be more truly the church God wills. The Baptist-Reformed international dialogue committee speaks for many when it asks, "Is not everyone ready to find his own opinion in the scripture? Therefore, . . . we must keep in close contact with Christians of other traditions; it is in the living interplay with them that we are mutually corrected."[14] In the past twenty years, the movement has also begun to realize that the interpretive community must be *humanly* expanded: we now generally agree that women, racial minorities, the poor, and others formerly excluded from the church's interpretive task must be included if Scripture is to disclose anything like the fullness of its riches. The WCC's statement entitled *Mission and Evangelism—An Ecumenical Affirmation* (1981) notes, "Today we are gratefully surprised by the insight and perspec-

13. Brown, *The Churches the Apostles Left Behind* (New York: Paulist Press, 1984), p. 149.
14. See *Growth in Agreement: Reports and Agreed Statements of Ecumenical Conversations on a World Level,* ed. Harding Meyer and Lukas Vischer (New York: Paulist Press, 1984), p. 136.

tive of the Gospel coming from the communities of the poor. They are discovering dimensions of the Gospel which have long been forgotten by the Church."[15] In this sense, "community" becomes an essential component of the search for "truth." One of the most important things about the Bible is the people with whom we read it. If we approach Scripture only within the perspective of our like-minded groupings, then we should not be surprised when others find our witness to be parochial.

Second, Christians need to acknowledge the diversity of Scripture while still seeking to identify the broad, central themes that run throughout the canon. Ecumenical conferences have accepted the fact that some portions of Scripture will have more significance for one church than for another. But they have also insisted that we dare exclude one another, or (more to the point) dare remain divided from one another, only on the basis of truly foundational themes.

This is the point where ecumenically minded Christians so often find fault with fundamentalists. The "five fundamentals"—the five overarching themes usually ascribed to by fundamentalist Christians—include the inerrancy of the Bible, the Virgin Birth, the deity of Jesus Christ, Christ's substitutionary atonement, and Christ's physical resurrection and future bodily return. Christians from other traditions might question whether the Virgin Birth, to take one example, is as foundational to the life of the church and as central to Scripture as the humanity of Jesus, the primacy of grace, the continuing activity of the Holy Spirit, the Trinity, the significance of the sacraments, or the command to love your neighbor as yourself—all missing from the fundamentalist checklist.[16]

Some of the debate is even more pointed. If American fundamentalist Jerry Falwell wants to use the Bible in politics, writes Martin Marty, then let him use the whole Bible: "For every inch in the Bible on pornography, there are 500 inches on poverty." According to Robert McAfee Brown, Falwell in his use of Scripture fails to recognize that he, too, interprets from a given perspective, one that "never subjects itself to the great biblical themes of doing justice or loving mercy, or acknowledging that God is truly Lord of all (even the Russians), or suggesting that peacemaking rather than warmaking might be an important task for believers."[17] Presumably these

15. *International Review of Mission,* Oct. 1982, p. 443.
16. See Avery Dulles, "Paths to Doctrinal Agreement: Ten Theses," *Theological Studies* 47 (1986): 34.
17. Brown, "Listen, Jerry Falwell!" *Christianity and Crisis,* 22 Dec. 1980, p. 364.

ecumenical spokespersons would also be willing to acknowledge that their list of favorite themes needs the challenge of alternative interpretations.

4. The fourth theological assumption behind the ecumenical vision (like the preceding three) deserves more attention than is possible to give it in this brief volume, but a few broad strokes may make the general point. As Christians we affirm that truth is less propositional than "personal," that, in fact, Jesus Christ is "the way, and the truth, and the life" (John 14:6). As Parker Palmer observes, when Pilate asks "What is truth?" (John 18:38), the word that betrays the inadequacy of his perspective is "what." Jesus claims not merely to teach the truth (though he does claim that—e.g., in John 8:40), but to embody it. Those who wish to know truth are invited into living relationship with him.[18]

How do we enter such relationship? The answer, as I understand it, is found in a key concept of Pauline theology (and of the ecumenical movement): *koinonia*. As used by Paul, *koinonia* means participation in (fellowship with) Christ *and* mutual participation in (fellowship with) the members of his body, the church. These two dimensions of Christian life—the "vertical" (Christ-centered) and the "horizontal" (human-centered)—simply cannot be separated. When someone does something to or for one of the least of these brothers and sisters, it is as if that person did it to or for Christ himself (Matt. 25).

Thus, to say that truth is "personal" is to say not that it is "subjective" but that it is "relational" (dialogical). It is to say that a deeper understanding of reality can be realized in the compassionate interaction of Christ's body, under the guidance of the Holy Spirit, who leads the community of Christ's followers in the gradual discovery of truth (John 16:13). Writes Palmer,

> His call to truth is a call to community—with him, with each other, with creation and its Creator. If what we know is an abstract, impersonal, apart from us, it cannot be truth, for truth involves a vulnerable, faithful, and risk-filled interpenetration of the knower and the known. Jesus calls Pilate out from behind his objectivism into a living relationship of truth. Pilate, taking refuge behind the impersonal objectivist "what," is unable to respond.[19]

The truth of God-in-Christ is not simply "out there" to be set forth in

18. Palmer, *To Know As We Are Known: A Spirituality of Education* (San Francisco: Harper & Row, 1983), p. 48.
19. Palmer, *To Know As We Are Known,* p. 49.

objective propositions (though Christians have an obligation to articulate their faith as clearly as possible), nor simply "in here" to be claimed as purely private perceptions. Rather, truth emerges in *koinonia*. For Christians, this is an epistemological principle. Saint Gregory wrote, "Love itself is knowledge; the more one loves the more one knows."[20] Ecumenical openness to genuine difference in Christian community is receptivity toward truth.

A corollary of this discussion, and an implication of our earlier discussion of diversity, is that some things claimed as "truths" by Christians are less essential (less involved with the disclosure in Christ of the sovereign and loving God) than others. One of the breakthroughs of modern ecumenism occurred when the Second Vatican Council penned the following words: "When comparing doctrines, [Catholic theologians] should remember that in Catholic teaching there exists an order or 'hierarchy' of truths, since they vary in their relationship to the foundation of the Christian faith."[21] In order to preserve the integrity of the community, consensus is needed on those things that are essential. But in order to preserve the loving openness of the community, diversity is needed on those things that are not essential. This means that we need not deny the "truth" of some of our traditional doctrines, practices, and structures to acknowledge that their universal acceptance is not necessary for renewed communion.

5. All of this helps us recognize that the ecumenical emphasis on the importance of the church and its unity is also, among other things, an epistemological principle. The diverse community of fellow Christians is an essential component of, and context for, the search for truth. Realizing that our interpretations of God's truth are partial, realizing that we are undeserving recipients of God's grace, not definitive possessors of it, we also realize that we need each other if we are serious about being the church God wills. Christianity does not provide absolute certainty about ultimate questions ("My ways are not your ways"); it offers a community of faith within which truth is sought and affirmed.

One tool for the common pursuit of truth in the church that has proved its worth over the past sixty years is "dialogue." An excellent illustration of the principle behind dialogue is offered by the literary critic Wayne Booth in his book entitled *Critical Understanding: The*

---

20. Saint Gregory, quoted by Palmer in *To Know As We Are Known*, p. 58.

21. Cited in *Doing the Truth in Charity*, ed. Thomas F. Stransky and John B. Sheerin (New York: Paulist Press, 1982), p. 26.

Powers and Limits of Pluralism. Booth invites his readers to imagine a cone that they observe without changing their basic angle of vision. Those who view the cone from below see a circle, something quite different from what is seen by those who view the cone from the side or the top. If you are serious about knowing what you are looking at, argues Booth, then (a) you need to look as carefully as possible from your particular angle, and (b) you need to share what you see with each other. We need not deny that the cone (i.e., truth) exists just because we cannot see it fully. And we need not deny that others see accurately from their perspectives in order to claim that a fuller vision is possible. In fact, we dare not caricature the other positions because a truer picture will demand that we really understand, see truly, what the others have seen—precisely the point of dialogue.[22]

Ecumenical dialogue is almost a spiritual orientation. This idea is expressed by Vatican II in a marvelous passage from the *Decree on Ecumenism:*

> There can be no ecumenism worthy of the name without a change of heart. For it is from newness of attitudes, from self-denial and unstinted love, that yearnings for unity take their rise and grow towards maturity. We should therefore pray to the divine Spirit for the grace to be genuinely self-denying, humble, gentle in the service of others, and to have an attitude of brotherly generosity towards them.[23]

If truth is the goal, then genuine repentance, willingness to be transformed, is essential. Through dialogue we are not building or renewing the church ourselves but attempting, imperfectly, to follow the leading of God's Spirit toward greater truth.

Beyond this, I want to suggest ten more specific guidelines for ecumenical dialogue. This list is by no means exhaustive or entirely original; it borrows heavily from similar "ground rules" proposed by Robert McAfee Brown and Leonard Swidler.[24] But it may prove useful at this juncture for thinking concretely about the church as a dialogical community.

i. Allow the other partners in dialogue to define themselves, to describe and witness to their faith in their own terms. Nothing under-

---

22. Booth, *Critical Understanding: The Powers and Limits of Pluralism* (Chicago: University of Chicago Press, 1979), p. 31.

23. *Decree on Ecumenism,* in *Doing the Truth in Charity,* p. 24.

24. See Brown, *The Ecumenical Revolution* (Garden City, N.Y.: Doubleday, 1969), pp. 70-79; and Swidler's foreword to *Jewish Monotheism and Christian Trinitarian Doctrine* by Pinchas Lapide and Jürgen Moltmann (Philadelphia: Fortress Press, 1981), pp. 7-15.

mines the common search for truth more quickly than stereotyping or caricaturing—which, after all, is a violation of the ninth commandment from Sinai: "You shall not bear false witness against your neighbor." This also implies that partners must be willing to revise their understanding of each other's faith and of the assumed points of disagreement between them in light of what they hear. This principle boils down to what might be called the Golden Rule of ecumenism: Try to understand others even as you hope to be understood by them. No church (or religion) wants to have another one define who it is.

ii. Have a clear understanding of your own faith and present it with complete honesty and sincerity. A Roman Catholic representative (to take an example from Brown) should be familiar with the documents of Vatican II as well as the Baltimore Catechism—and be willing to discuss weaknesses as well as strengths. There is a corollary principle that needs to be emphasized. Meaningful dialogue occurs when the people involved not only are knowledgeable about their faith but are committed to it, when what they believe provides fundamental orientation and motivation for their lives. Otherwise, why bother?

iii. Acknowledge, as I have stressed all along, that genuine dialogue rests on a common devotion to truth. Conversations aimed at fact-finding or at teaching the other party or at building more cordial relations have their place, but they are not dialogue as the ecumenical movement conceives of it. Another way to say this is that dialogue should encourage mutual growth. In his book *Christian Tolerance,* Robert Jewett identifies three strategies advocated by Paul in his letter to the Romans for achieving a diverse yet truth-oriented community: (1) protect the integrity of your adversaries (an idea that surely includes allowing them to define themselves), (2) protect your own integrity (i.e., know your own faith and present it honestly), and (3) encourage common growth. The aggressive campaigns of the Jewish and Hellenistic Christians were to give way to peace in Christ. Yet such peace, writes Jewett, was not to be static but built on the assumption that each side had a responsibility for the other. "The mutually nurturing community is thus the ultimate expression of genuine tolerance."[25]

iv. Recognize that dialogue is between people and not just between churches or ideological positions. This is a basic principle behind the work of the WCC's department on "Dialogue with *People* of

25. Jewett, *Christian Tolerance,* p. 139.

Living Faiths"[26] (italics mine), but it also has an important application to intra-Christian discussion. To know one's neighbor in the act of believing, to ask what God may be doing in his or her life, is a very different experience from knowing that belief as an abstract doctrine. Even if we are convinced in all good faith that the other is wrong, there is a considerable difference between rejecting an impersonal doctrine and relating to a "mistaken" fellow Christian.

v. Be sure to dialogue with contemporary partners. To take only one example, members of my denomination, the Christian Church (Disciples of Christ), frequently seem to reject the idea of bishops on the basis of authoritarian images derived from eighteenth-century Anglicanism or pre–Vatican II Roman Catholicism.

vi. Be willing to separate essentials from nonessentials and to require agreement only on the former. This follows, of course, from all that we have been saying about diversity and the "hierarchy of truth." Dialogue should try to determine which issues demand consensus if we are to know that we worship and serve the same Jesus Christ, and which issues do not.

vii. Do not require more agreement from your partners in dialogue than you require from members of your own communion. There is a legitimate concern that the results of dialogue will have less or different significance in another church context than they have in one's own, but the demand for absolute precision or for consensus that is too extensive betrays a lack of trust that is deadly for genuine dialogue.

viii. Interpret the faith of the dialogue partner in its best rather than in its worst light. Brown makes this point forcefully when he argues that "if Protestants want to be appraised in terms of Reinhold Niebuhr rather than Carl McIntire, they must be willing to evaluate the papacy in terms of John XXIII rather than the Borgias."[27] The point is that we witness to and celebrate the riches of both traditions (both part of the great Christian heritage), not emphasize the poverty of our neighbors.

ix. Deal openly with the hard issues as well as those on which easier agreement is possible. Dialogue committed to truth is not served by falsely conciliatory attitudes any more than it is served by a dogged insistence on emphasizing areas of divergence. Samuel McCrea Cavert, a well-known Protestant ecumenist, expresses it well: "When we are trying to see things through the eyes of another,

26. See *Guidelines on Dialogue* (Geneva: World Council of Churches, 1979).
27. Brown, *The Ecumenical Revolution*, p. 74.

we may be tempted to be so amiable that our differences are obscured or blurred. For genuine and fruitful dialogue, candor is as essential as respect." Actually, it may not be wise to tackle the thorniest issues at the outset. There is good reason to begin with those questions on which there is more common ground and from which trust can grow. But gradually, as trust deepens, the more difficult issues should emerge.

x. Search for ways to turn the increased understanding achieved through dialogue into activities for renewal. The acid test of a true desire for Christian unity, writes Catholic theologian Hans Küng, is "the willingness to renew our own church by fulfilling the justified request of other churches."[28] Without this there can be no serious pursuit of truth.

I want to make two additional remarks about the church as a community of dialogue. First, it must be said that there are times when dialogue is inappropriate or impossible: for example, when the disparity in power between the would-be "partners" is so great (e.g., between a dictator and subjects) that it could in no sense be a dialogue between equals, or when one side claims all truth in advance or announces in advance its unwillingness to change regardless of what is said during the dialogue, or when one party can in no way recognize elements of the church in the other. That brings us back, of course, to our central question about the limits of acceptable diversity. For now, however, I want simply to maintain that those limits are drawn—that dialogue is broken between groups professing to be Christian—only as the extreme exception and not as the rule.

It has recently become fashionable for liberal scholars to attack dialogue. All it does, they contend, is buttress the status quo because participants talk about unjust realities instead of actively seeking to change them. To take one frequently used example, we do not need more dialogue about the role of women in the church (the entrenched men are happy enough to keep talking about it); what we need is more overt resistance to patriarchal structures. These concerns are important. Dialogue has undoubtedly been misused, and there are limits to its application. But the points made earlier in this chapter lead me to contend that these limits are approached only reluctantly. Since dialogue challenges the presuppositions of *all* parties involved, it will always be suspect in the eyes of those—reformers and status-quo defenders alike—who are convinced that all truth is on their side. That alone should make us wary of its dismissal. Beyond that, dia-

28. Küng, *The Church* (Garden City, N.Y.: Image Books, 1976), p. 373.

logue, properly understood, *can* be an effective tool for promoting change. The renewal of the church brought about through dialogue over the past two generations is evidence that supports this claim. We will return to this difficult issue in Chapter IV.

Second, if truth is the goal, then the church must be open to the possibility that the painstaking results of dialogue will themselves be disrupted (as all of our temporary unities must be disrupted) for the sake of greater obedience to God's will. Dialogue, after all, is a principle of relationship, not an isolated, one-time event. To state this another way, the church lives in the tension between memory and anticipation, between apostolic Tradition and eschatological fulfillment. Thus, on the one hand, the ecumenical movement has insisted that expanding the community of interpreters means listening to the church across time as well as space and acknowledging the importance of continuity in faith. But, on the other hand, the ecumenical movement has also insisted that God *can* do a new thing and that the church we are called to be is not synonymous with the church we have been. In short, the movement has sought to appropriate the "catholic substance," the whole apostolic Tradition, on the basis of the "protestant principle" that the church must be ever renewed. It seeks both a recovery of wholeness and a movement toward greater faithfulness. Truth, it affirms, is discovered in the past witness to God's revelation in Christ, but it is also found in the community's present encounter with the living Word, and will be more fully revealed at that time when we shall see clearly, not through a glass darkly.

THE REJECTION OF IDOLATRY

I want to conclude this discussion of theological foundations, and to foreshadow the next three chapters, by suggesting that the ecumenical vision can appropriately be construed as a rejection of idolatry. As I see it, the ecumenical movement, though it seldom uses this terminology, has been particularly concerned with three forms of idolatry.

First, there is the idolatry of humans claiming absolute knowledge of God's will. As I have already argued at some length, confusing humanly constructed images or concepts with God is denounced throughout Scripture—though that has not kept Christians from repeatedly doing so.

Second, there is the idolatry of being so conformed to the world's divisions that we allow the church, the body of Christ, to reflect them. "We have failed," said the Amsterdam Assembly in 1948, "be-

cause we ourselves [i.e., the churches] have been partakers in man's
disorder."[29]

The apostle Paul provides precedent for this charge. In Corinth
the church had split into factions, each taking the name of a leader.
"The names of Peter, Apollos, and [Paul]," writes Hendrik Berkhof,
"came for many to be ideologies or powers, by which they oriented
their belief and life."[30] Paul reverses the genitive. Do not say, "I am
Paul's" or "I am of Apollos." You are Christ's and, therefore,
"whether Paul or Apollos . . . or the world or life or death or the
present or the future, all are yours" (1 Cor. 3:21-23). Elsewhere in
Chapter 3 (vss. 1-4), Paul tells the believers of Corinth that their divisions show that they are still "carnal," still "all-too-human," by which
he means that when Christians begin to gather in groups that glory in
the things which separate them, then they are falling from the life of
the Spirit to the life of the flesh. They are falling back into the old
world where people are drawn together and pushed apart by human
teachings instead of living in the new world where they realize that
Christ is all and that genuine community is possible only through
mutual commitment to him. Fundamental allegiance to a part (Paul or
Apollos, Methodist or Roman Catholic) instead of the whole (Christ)
is simply idolatry.

One of the most scathing attacks on this tendency to be found in
modern theological literature is that of H. Richard Niebuhr in his
book entitled *The Social Sources of Denominationalism*. It deserves
to be quoted at length. A divided church, claims Niebuhr, represents

> the accommodation of Christianity to the caste-system of
> human society. It carries over into the organization of the
> Christian principle of brotherhood the prides and prejudices,
> the privilege and prestige, the injustices and inequalities of
> that specious order of high and low wherein men find the
> satisfaction of their craving for vainglory. The division of the
> churches closely follows the division of men into the castes of
> national, racial, and economic groups. It draws the color line
> in the church of God; it fosters the misunderstandings, the
> self-exaltations, the hatreds of jingoistic nationalism by con-
> tinuing in the body of Christ the spurious differences of pro-
> vincial loyalties; it seats the rich and poor apart at the table of
> the Lord, where the fortunate may enjoy the bounty they

29. See *The First Assembly of the World Council of Churches*, ed. W. A.
Visser 't Hooft (New York: Harper, 1949).

30. Berkhof, *Christ and the Powers*, trans. John H. Yoder (Scottdale, Pa.:
Herald Press, 1962), p. 77.

have provided while the others feed upon the crusts their poverty affords.[31]

The church shows its conformity to the world in numerous ways: denominationalism, which is the organizational form of "religious freedom" enshrined in the American Constitution's separation of church and state; "localism," which identifies Christian community with the needs and preferences of a particular location or social group instead of seeing it in the context of the *oikoumene*, "the whole inhabited earth"; traditional patterns of interchurch aid that imitate the paternalistic attitudes of wealthy nations by dividing the body of Christ into "donors" and "receivers"; discrimination in the church based on race or sex. "If the tensions of the world cannot be faced honestly in the Church itself and at least a start made to overcome them by penitence," writes WCC staff member Ulrich Duchrow, "there can be no firm basis for the Church to turn its eyes to the world itself."[32]

Yes, there is a commitment to the fullness of truth that makes us wary of "easy unity," but there is also a truth about our oneness in Christ that should make us wary of succumbing to the artificial barriers of human society, of allowing worldly patterns rather than Christ to determine the shape of our common life. To the extent this happens, the church becomes less truly the church. Ernst Lange, in his remarkable book about the ecumenical movement entitled *And Yet It Moves,* goes even further. This movement, he contends, is "the most massive domestic Christian protest against the way Christianity, by its alliance with the powers that be, [has] been transformed into its exact opposite."[33]

That leads us to the third form of idolatry: that of denying Christ's lordship in favor of other gods, or of refusing to assert Christ's lordship in the face of other gods. In his study for the British Council of Churches, published by the WCC as *The Other Side of 1984,* Lesslie Newbigin contends that, if the current North Atlantic church were transferred to first-century or second-century Rome, the Empire would not bother to persecute it.[34] Rome easily embraced

31. Niebuhr, *The Social Sources of Denominationalism* (New York: Henry Holt, 1929), p. 6.

32. Duchrow, *Conflict over the Ecumenical Movement,* trans. David Lewis (Geneva: World Council of Churches, 1981), p. 148.

33. Lange, *And Yet It Moves: Dream and Reality of the Ecumenical Movement,* trans. Edwin Robertson (Grand Rapids: Eerdmans, 1979), p. 5.

34. Newbigin, *The Other Side of 1984* (Geneva: World Council of Churches, 1983), pp. 32ff.

various cults aimed at promoting the personal salvation of their members; what it could not tolerate was a community called into existence by the good news that God, incarnate in Jesus Christ, is Lord of all creation, the One to whom alone ultimate allegiance is due. Churches today have become precisely what the early church refused to be: "religious fraternities" *(thiasoi* or *heranoi)*, and competing ones at that, offering visions of personal blessedness in another world. If the question behind the ecumenical movement is really "What does it mean to be the church God wills?" then that movement must help the church become once more the *ekklesia* (public assembly) that challenges the gods of this world with its proclamation of a "kingdom" of justice and peace. In Newbigin's words, "The struggle for Christian unity cannot be severed from the recovery of a genuinely missionary confrontation with our so-called modern culture, in which the Church will be seen again as the *ecclesia tou Theou,* the Assembly to which God summons all peoples and in which no other sovereignty is recognized but his."[35]

Needless to say, there are many Christians, especially in North America, who reject this perspective, attacking the WCC and other instruments of the ecumenical movement for their "political involvements." I will argue later in this book that Christians may well disagree on particular courses of public action, but even conservative Christian scholars are increasingly acknowledging that Scripture shows us a community inevitably at odds with the world's powers and principalities. According to Stanley Hauerwas and William Willimon, it is hard to escape the conclusion "that the Christian faith is intellectually 'imperialistic,' a contentious competitor with all other claimants for truth."[36] The fact that we know our perceptions of truth to be partial, in need of mutual correction, should not prevent us from challenging the pretensions of Caesar with a resolute "No!" in the name of the one, sovereign God. "Hitler had no objections to Christians who confessed that Jesus is Lord," Arthur Cochrane observes in his excellent study entitled *The Church's Confession under Hitler,* "but he was enraged when they confessed that Jesus is Lord and Hitler is not."[37] There are times when we cannot indulge in innocu-

35. Newbigin, "The Basis and Forms of Unity," *Midstream,* Jan. 1984, p. 12.

36. Hauerwas and Willimon, "Embarrassed by the Presence of God," *Christian Century,* 30 Jan. 1985, p. 99.

37. Cochrane, *The Church's Confession under Hitler* (Philadelphia: Westminster Press, 1962), p. 211.

ous affirmations but must firmly reject some of the world's diversities for the sake of truth and love.

Robin Scroggs summarizes his study of Pauline theology this way: "The church is not prohibited from entering the world; the world is excluded from entering the church."[38] But the contemporary church often lives in precisely the reverse way, structuring its life according to the divisions of the world while resisting the notion that the church should engage in "worldly" debate and struggle.

It is at this point that we can begin to see the integration of the ecumenical vision, the insight which holds together the impulses represented by the Faith and Order Movement and the Life and Work Movement: The church proclaims the truth of God, and thus challenges other truths, not just by what it does, and not just by the purity of its doctrinal formulations, but by what it is. Professor Berkhof, a leading figure in the ecumenical movement for many years, may have said it best in his classic little volume called *Christ and the Powers*:

> The very existence of the church, in which Gentiles and Jews, who heretofore walked according to the *stoicheia* [powers] of the world, live together in Christ's fellowship, is itself a proclamation, a sign, a token to the Powers that their unbroken dominion has come to an end. . . . All resistance and every attack against the gods of this age will be unfruitful, unless the church herself *is* resistance and attack, unless she demonstrates in her life and fellowship how men can live freed from the Powers [e.g., Mammon, nationalism, racism, and other forms of social injustice].[39]

In its refusal to tolerate many of the walls erected over the centuries between people confessing Jesus Christ, the ecumenical movement wants not to compromise truth but to repudiate idolatry through the visible embodiment of *shalom*. It is saying that lines need to be drawn, but that we have often drawn them in the wrong places. It is saying that our willingness to break fellowship over different interpretations of justification or the sacraments, along with our unwillingness to challenge worldly values in the name of that in which our common identity is rooted (the sovereignty of God and the lordship of Christ), is a betrayal of the New Testament church. It is saying, in short, that the church today—divided and compromised by the powers it is called to expose—is not the church God calls us to be.

38. Scroggs, *Paul for a New Day* (Philadelphia: Fortress Press, 1977), p. 52.

39. Berkhof, *Christ and the Powers*, p. 51.

CHAPTER III

DOCTRINAL DIVERSITY: HOW MUCH DIVERSITY IS ACCEPTABLE WITH REGARD TO SACRAMENTS AND MINISTRY?

Who is a proper candidate for baptism? Is Christ really present in the eucharist (what some traditions prefer to call the Lord's Supper or Holy Communion)? How does the church indicate and maintain its continuity with the faith of the early apostles? Where are decisions about the church (its mission and witness, the truth of its preaching) actually made?

Questions such as these have divided parts of the church for nearly one thousand years, and since the sixteenth century have split Protestants from Roman Catholics, and Protestants from other Protestants. Any movement aimed at promoting the unity of the church will certainly need to deal with such traditionally sticky issues. The sorry fact is that Christians are unable to join as the whole church around the Lord's Table, are unable mutually to recognize their ministries as true ministries of Word and sacrament, and, in some cases, continue to rebaptize individuals baptized in another Christian tradition. These are quite obviously examples not of diversity but of division, and they obscure our visible witness as the one body of Christ.

The good news of this chapter is that the ecumenical movement has been dealing with these divisions, and with greater success than most ecumenists would have dreamed possible just a generation ago. The past decade has witnessed few church unions (e.g., such as that which produced the United Church of Christ in 1957) for reasons we will explore in Chapter V, but it has seen absolutely remarkable, unprecedented convergence on a lengthy list of doctrinal disputes. Several examples, drawn from different types of dialogue, may give a sense of the achievement and momentum.

38

The Anglican–Roman Catholic International Commission (ARCIC) completed fourteen years of work in 1981 by announcing that it had reached "substantial agreement" on the eucharist, ministry, and authority in the church. ARCIC is only the most advanced of a host of international "bilateral" (two-party) theological conversations aimed at "overcoming theological and ecclesiastical divergences inherited from the past"[1] in order to build theological foundations for deeper fellowship between globally organized confessional families. The important volume entitled *Growth in Agreement,* edited by Harding Meyer and Lukas Vischer, contains major reports from twelve such conversations, seven of them involving the Roman Catholic Church as an official partner. Other communions involved in international dialogues include the Anglican, Baptist, Disciples, Eastern Orthodox, Lutheran, Methodist, Old Catholic, Oriental Orthodox, Pentecostal, and Reformed.

In the United States, theologians representing three Lutheran churches (now united in the Evangelical Lutheran Church in America) and the Roman Catholic Church have reached fundamental accord, after five years of dialogue, on the doctrine of justification (the one issue most central to Luther's dispute with Rome). Another American "bilateral" dialogue has resulted in occasional eucharistic sharing between these same Lutheran churches and the Episcopal Church. A bibliography of interconfessional two-party dialogues, published by the Centro Pro Unione in Rome, lists more than eighty of these at the national level in various parts of the world.

The American Consultation on Church Union (COCU) capped twenty-five years of trust-building with the publication in 1985 of the *COCU Consensus,* a document that details the theological agreement on membership, worship, ministry, confession of faith, and the nature of the church achieved by theologians representing nine Protestant denominations. The hope is that this common theological statement, if endorsed by the participating churches, will serve as the basis of a "covenant" form of unity. Similar work is going on in other parts of the world, Wales being perhaps the most advanced example.

I have saved what may be the best for last. The WCC's document entitled *Baptism, Eucharist and Ministry (BEM)*[2] is now widely re-

---

1. *Growth in Agreement: Reports and Agreed Statements of Ecumenical Conversations on a World Level,* ed. Harding Meyer and Lukas Vischer (New York: Paulist Press, 1984), p. 4.

2. *Baptism, Eucharist and Ministry* (Geneva: World Council of Churches, 1983). Subsequent references to this source will be made parenthetically in the text.

garded as the most significant theological achievement of the modern ecumenical movement, generating an unprecedented amount of interest both here and abroad. One big reason for such attention is that *BEM* is the result of a truly expanded community of interpreters. The body that produced this text, the Faith and Order Commission of the WCC, includes Anglicans, Baptists, Disciples, Eastern Orthodox believers, Lutherans, Methodists, Old Catholics, Oriental Orthodox believers, Presbyterians (Reformed), and Roman Catholics, as well as representatives from various United, Pentecostal, and Anabaptist churches. And the members come from six continents. There is simply no more confessionally and culturally comprehensive theological forum in the Christian world, which makes the convergence Faith and Order has produced all the more impressive.

In this chapter I propose to focus my attention on *BEM*, asking what this text and the process surrounding it can teach us about *where* the ecumenical movement is drawing the limits of acceptable diversity on traditionally divisive doctrinal questions and about *how* such limits are being drawn. After looking at *BEM* specifically, I will end the chapter by offering five general propositions regarding the wider process of doctrinal reconciliation.

READING BETWEEN THE LINES OF *BEM*

It seems clear that unity, whatever else it might entail, would be meaningless if it did not enable people baptized in different places to recognize one another mutually as having been incorporated into the one, universal church; it would be hollow if Christians still found themselves excluded from some celebrations of Holy Communion; and it would be incomplete if those ordained in certain communities were not acknowledged by all to be exercising valid ministries of word and sacrament. These visible signs of brokenness are no problem for those who are convinced that the boundaries of the true church of Jesus Christ go no further than their community and those whose baptism and ministry they recognize and with whom they have regular eucharistic fellowship. The ecumenical movement, however, is built on the conviction that the church extends further than most of our churches have been officially willing to admit; that, despite our rebaptisms and reordinations and effective excommunication, these others are *Christians* whose diverse practices and theologies do not mean that they are severed from the body of Christ. As Robert McAfee Brown puts it, the emphasis, even for relatively open-minded believers, used to be on *separated* brothers and sisters; now it is on separated *brothers and sisters*.[3] We *ought* to be able to say with these partners in dialogue that we have one baptism, one table, one ministry.

Because baptism, eucharist, and ministry constitute such visible signs of our separation, they have been the focus of theological attention since the First Conference on Faith and Order in 1927. But it was not until the 1960s that a text containing the theological convergence achieved through decades of dialogue began to take shape. This text was shared with member churches of the WCC (and others represented in Faith and Order) after the Nairobi Assembly in 1975, and suggestions from the 150 responses, as well as the results of various specialized conferences, were incorporated into the developing document. Finally, at their 1982 meeting in Lima, Peru, the members of the WCC's Faith and Order Commission were asked a critical question: Has this text reached sufficient "maturity" (is there a sufficient area of agreement, sufficient evidence of convergence) that it should be transmitted to the churches for "official response" and "reception"? The answer was—astonishingly—a unanimous "yes."[4]

Two aspects of this process are particularly relevant to our concern. First, it must always be stressed that neither Faith and Order nor the WCC as a whole "approved" *BEM*. The WCC has repeatedly affirmed that it cannot legislate doctrinal agreement for its member churches. The emphasis on official response (due in Geneva by the end of 1985) and long-term reception is a way of saying that only the churches themselves can determine whether *BEM* falls within the range of acceptable diversity, and could, therefore, serve as a basis of deeper fellowship for those churches that mutually affirm it. The theologians have said, in effect, that they have done their work; now it is up to the churches to draw the consequences of the achieved convergence.

Second, one of the questions posed by Faith and Order to the churches is of special significance: To what extent can your church recognize in this text the faith of the church through the ages? In other words, churches are being asked to evaluate *BEM* not as a

3. Brown, *The Ecumenical Revolution* (Garden City, N.Y.: Doubleday, 1969), p. 72.

4. There are numerous resources available that describe the process surrounding *BEM* and offer critical assessment of it, including my *Why It Matters* (Geneva: World Council of Churches, 1985) and *Ecumenical Perspectives on Baptism, Eucharist and Ministry,* ed. Max Thurian (Geneva: World Council of Churches, 1982).

clever compromise or as a useful description of what some traditions have believed, but as an expression of Christian truth. But it is precisely this commitment to the full truth of the gospel that should make the churches most wary of evaluating *BEM* simply by their confessional yardsticks, each of which (as I have already argued) is inevitably partial and conditioned by the historical and geographical circumstances in which it was uttered. We have a right and a responsibility to ask how well our theologians have done their job, but we also have an obligation to measure, whenever possible, our traditions by the theology and practice of the universal church. Once we accept the fact that truth is not served by a defensive clinging to confessional heritage, we are freed to treat *BEM* as a source of renewal rather than as a threat to cherished identity.

With these introductory points in mind, I will turn now to the text itself. This is by no means a systematic study of *BEM;* numerous study guides and commentaries are available for that purpose. Rather, I want to make six observations that show some of the methodological assumptions behind this document. In this way, the treatment of diversity and truth in *BEM* may begin to emerge. To simplify the task, I will concentrate for now on baptism and the eucharist.

1. Crucial to *BEM's* successful convergence is the attempt to hold in tension theological affirmations that the churches have often split apart or weighted too heavily in one direction. The linchpin of the baptism section, for example, is the statement that "Baptism is both God's gift and our human response to that gift" (B8). In this act, grace and faith—the objective, universal work of God through the Spirit and our personal appropriation of its benefits through trusting response—are inseparably linked. To put it another way, baptism is not a magic ritual but the worshipful celebration of a believing community, but in that context it is a means of grace in which we pray for the transforming presence of the Holy Spirit with confidence that God will answer that prayer. Thus *BEM* can speak of baptism as "a gift of God" and "a work of the Holy Spirit" as well as "a rite of commitment" that implies "confession of sin and conversion of heart." While different traditions may emphasize one pole or the other, the ecumenical convergence insists that either/or arguments do not do justice to the full witness of Scripture and Tradition.

Similarly, the heart of the eucharist section is a more biblical understanding of *anamnesis* or "memorial." The sterile impasse over whether the eucharist is a sacrament of Christ's "real presence" ("This is my body") or a memorial of his death and resurrection ("Do this in remembrance of me") has been overcome, at least to a great extent, through recent scholarship. What the ecumenical convergence affirms is that memorial—when set in the context of proclamation, thanksgiving, and invocation of the Holy Spirit—is to be understood not as a pleasant recollection of something that happened "back then" or "over there," but as a way of making the reality of God's saving act in Christ newly present for each generation. "The biblical idea of memorial as applied to the eucharist," *BEM* asserts, "refers to this present efficacy of God's work when it is celebrated by God's people in a liturgy. Christ himself with all that he has accomplished for us and for all creation . . . is present in this *anamnesis,* granting us communion with himself" (E6). Once again it is not either/or; "memorial" and "real presence" go hand in hand.

2. This first methodological principle points in the direction of a second: *BEM* attempts to recover more of the rich biblical diversity than our individual traditions have generally been willing to acknowledge. Scripture, it says, confronts us with multiple images—participation in Christ's death and resurrection, the washing away of sin, renewal and new birth, exodus from bondage—which nevertheless point to a single reality. An admirable summary of this ecumenical approach is found in the *COCU Consensus* (which closely parallels *BEM* on many of these issues):

> The act of baptism effects, or signifies, the incorporation of the baptized in Christ's death and resurrection (Romans 6:11; Colossians 2:11-15), makes them living members of the Church universal (1 Corinthians 12:13), and by the power of the Holy Spirit enables them to confess their faith, to renounce sin and overcome death (Acts 2:38; Romans 6:8), and in their new identity to commit themselves in a new life and ministry of love and righteousness, which are a foretaste here and now of the life of the Kingdom (Ephesians 1:13-14).[5]

An exclusive focus on one or two of these meanings would be a truncation of the scriptural witness.

The same can be said of *BEM's* section on the eucharist, where that sacramental meal is spoken of as (a) a thanksgiving to the Father, (b) a memorial of Christ, (c) an invocation of the Spirit (note the Trinitarian character of the text), (d) a communion of the faithful, and (e) a vision and foretaste of the kingdom. No single theme, *BEM* suggests, does justice to our experience or the biblical record.

5. *COCU Consensus* (Philadelphia: Consultation on Church Union, 1985), p. 36.

However, *BEM* does not rely on Scripture as its sole authority. Indeed, Faith and Order, at its 1963 Montreal conference, acknowledged that Scripture and Tradition are inseparably bound; neither one is authoritative by itself. The Bible is embedded in Tradition, written by the early church and interpreted by the church in each succeeding generation. Tradition, for its part, is not a collection of static tenets but the living reality of God's revelation in Christ, passed on in the community of the faithful and always measured by the plumb line of the apostolic witness as recorded in Scripture. Thus Faith and Order described the norm of the church's proclamation as "the Tradition of the Gospel, testified in Scripture, transmitted in and by the Church through the power of the Holy Spirit."[6]

This discussion of authority becomes particularly important when dealing with "rebaptism." Some churches reject the idea of rebaptism but still immerse those adults who come to them having been sprinkled in infancy. Those churches generally regard Scripture as the sole and unambiguous authority for theological proclamation, and they claim to find no biblical warrant for baptizing babies. The ecumenical response, as suggested in *BEM* (B11), takes two forms: first, while "baptism upon personal profession of faith is the most clearly attested pattern in the New Testament documents," the biblical evidence is not unambiguous; and second, Tradition shows the church moving in new directions for valid reasons. Most baptisms in the apostolic era were undoubtedly—and inevitably—of adult converts. But once believing parents began to bring their children into the community, new theological understandings of God's gracious activity began to emerge.

3. In line with our discussion of dialogue, *BEM* attempts to separate those issues that are primary (and thus require clear agreement) from those that are secondary (on which diversity is to be welcomed). The mode of baptism is a good example. *BEM* takes a strong stand that baptism is administered with water in the name of the Triune God, and that it should be celebrated in public worship. The text also suggests that immersion can be a powerful sign of participation in Christ's death and resurrection, but it is clear that *BEM* regards the amount of water used to be a secondary issue (B17 and B18).

Another, perhaps more controversial example has to do with the way Christ's real presence is related to the eucharistic elements. Some churches, of course, maintain doctrinally that the presence is to be understood, in some way, as a transformation of the bread and

6. *The Fourth World Conference on Faith and Order,* ed. P. C. Rodger and Lukas Vischer (New York: Association Press, 1964), p. 52.

wine; others affirm real presence but do not link it so directly with the elements. *BEM* simply points to this diversity in a commentary (E13) and says that it is now up to the churches to decide if they can live with these theological perspectives in one fellowship. What is primary is the affirmation that the eucharist is a uniquely effective means for realizing communion with Christ. The explanation of how this happens is a mystery beyond full expression on which some diversity is appropriate.

4. *BEM* seems deliberately to emphasize certain themes because they counter popular misunderstandings or restore needed balance to the church's sacramental theology. For example, the whole document is permeated with an unusually strong emphasis (at least for the Western churches) on the activity of the Holy Spirit. It is the Spirit "who makes the historical words of Jesus present and alive. Being assured by Jesus' promise in the words of institution that it will be answered, the Church prays to the Father for the gift of the Holy Spirit in order that the eucharistic event may be a reality" (E14). The intent is not simply to pacify the Eastern churches but to stress that the eucharist is not a magic act (something we do). It is, rather, an expression of faith that God, through the Spirit, will act to answer our prayer for the fellowship promised by Christ.

The authors of *BEM* were obviously also aware that nearly all traditions, at one time or another, have allowed both sacraments to be seen as private, individualistic acts, as something that happens "between me and God" that has little to do with the person in the next pew, let alone those outside the sanctuary. This is most definitely not the spirit of *BEM*. It regards both baptism and the Lord's Supper as basic bonds of unity among Christians that should, therefore, always be celebrated corporately. So pervasive is this orientation that Ernst Lange referred to an earlier draft of the text as "an unmistakable 'readaptation' of the sacraments," one that emphasizes their social— as well as eschatological, ethical, and missionary—significance.[7]

5. *BEM* frequently tries to get beyond old controversies by setting them in a different or larger context. For instance, the gap between believers' baptism and infant baptism is bridged by speaking of baptism as part of a process of Christian nurture that includes (a) the growth of the child within a supportive Christian community, (b) a personal, public confession of faith at an appropriate age, and (c) faithful discipleship throughout one's life (B12). Indeed, the text implies, there are not two types of baptism but two distinctive mo-

7. Lange, *And Yet It Moves: Dream and Reality of the Ecumenical Movement,* trans. Edwin Robertson (Grand Rapids: Eerdmans, 1979), p. 48.

ments at which individuals may experience the one baptism that is both gift and response. By emphasizing one moment or the other, churches have often unduly minimized other aspects of the nurturing process.

Another example is the way *BEM* sets eucharistic "sacrifice" within the context of the church as a community of intercession. *BEM* expresses the broad agreement that Christ's death on the cross is unrepeatable; there should be no talk of a literal reenactment of his unique sacrifice through which we have received the promise of forgiveness and newness of life. This promise, however, is made actual each time we celebrate the sacred meal, allowing us to pray through Christ for God's blessing on the world. It is in this way, says *BEM,* that references in Roman Catholic theology to the eucharist as "propitiatory sacrifice" may be understood (E8 and commentary).

6. As a last illustration of *BEM's* methodology, the text refuses to separate theology into neat compartments marked "sacraments" and "ethics," or "mission" and "doctrine." It points in the direction of contemporary confession by insisting, with some of its most "uncompromising" language, that these be held together:

> The eucharistic celebration demands reconciliation and sharing among all those regarded as brothers and sisters in the one family of God and is a constant challenge in the search for appropriate relationships in social, economic and political life. All kinds of injustice, racism, separation and lack of freedom are radically challenged when we share in the body and blood of Christ. (E20)

> Baptism, as a baptism into Christ's death, has ethical implications which not only call for personal sanctification, but also motivate Christians to strive for the realization of the will of God in all realms of life. (B10)

Much of this, it seems to me, is intended to show that old battle lines have shifted. Believers' churches, for example, once found it necessary to speak of the church as a voluntary society of those who have heard the gospel with faith and commit themselves at the time of baptism to a life of discipleship. Believers' churches took this tack in order to counter the "official churches" with their hordes of apparently lukewarm, though baptized, members. By now, however, we have surely learned that the baptism of those able to make a confession of faith can still produce generations of tepid culture-religionists, while the baptism of infants can be powerfully understood as the proleptic beginning of a life of mission. The point is that *all* churches are in need of renewal. We can acknowledge that many past divisions may now show themselves to be legitimate diversities as long as we also acknowledge that all churches are in need of transformation toward greater faithfulness.

It is time to summarize by reading between the lines. *BEM,* as I understand it, expresses at least two general limits on the diversity the church can responsibly tolerate. First, foundational to *BEM,* and to all the work of Faith and Order of which I am aware, are affirmations about Christ and the Trinity that are derived from the conciliar definitions of Nicea-Constantinople and Chalcedon, expressed in the first paragraph of the WCC's constitution and repeated in the preface to *BEM.* As stated in its constitution, the WCC is a "fellowship of churches which confess the Lord Jesus Christ as God and Saviour according to the Scriptures and therefore seek to fulfill together their common calling to the glory of the one God, Father, Son and Holy Spirit." *BEM* is filled with paragraphs that acknowledge the Triune character of God as well as paragraphs that speak of Christ as the incarnate Son of God (E14), the crucified and risen Lord of the church and the world (B1), the Liberator of all human beings (B4), the Suffering Servant who proclaims and enacts the presence of the kingdom by his teachings and signs (E4), and the presently active High Priest and Intercessor (E8). In short, the Trinity and the lordship of Jesus Christ, "truly God and truly man," are presuppositions of the entire work, presuppositions on which genuine diversity would not be possible. The central place given these doctrines would also seem to be consistent with the thinking of the Second Vatican Council. Immediately after suggesting that there is a "hierarchy of truths," the *Decree on Ecumenism* urges all Christians to confess "before the whole world . . . their faith in God, one and three, in the incarnate Son of God, our Redeemer and Lord."[8]

Second, as already mentioned, *BEM's* attempt to hold together theological polarities indicates that, while different emphases are legitimate, undervaluing either pole is not. Several of these polarities have been dealt with in the preceding paragraphs: grace and faith, Scripture and Tradition, sacrament and mission, the individual and the corporate body (Christian nurture, for example, requires personal decision undertaken within the context of the church). One further example may help to clarify this approach. Our sacramental life, says *BEM,* involves a tension between memory and anticipation, tradition

8. *Decree on Ecumenism,* in *Doing the Truth in Charity,* ed. Thomas F. Stransky and John B. Sheerin (New York: Paulist Press, 1982), p. 26.

and eschatology. Paragraph E3 in the eucharist section notes that Holy Communion is an offering of thanks "for everything accomplished by God" and "for everything that God will accomplish." This same tension is found, of course, in the institution narratives themselves. We eat and drink in remembrance of Christ and in anticipation of the day when we will feast with him in his kingdom. We celebrate what God has done for our salvation, but our celebration is tinged with restlessness: Come, Lord Jesus! There is too much injustice. Therefore, come in the fullness of your reign. It is the insistence on this *tension*—this "both-and"—that gives *BEM's* treatment of the sacraments much of its ethical thrust.

Before speaking about the church response to *BEM,* I want to respond myself to a possible misperception. My purpose in the previous pages has not been to offer an apology for this particular document. There are several paragraphs that I personally wish had been written differently, and in my opinion the churches have offered numerous suggestions in their responses that could strengthen the convergence *BEM* represents. That is as it should be. Like any ecumenical text, *BEM* is nothing more than a tool for helping us to move toward the living communion of trust, sharing, and common service *(koinonia)* that we seek to make ever more manifest. What I have wanted to show, however, is that *BEM* attempts *both* to embrace a wide range of acceptable diversity *and* to impose limits on such diversity. The methods used in *BEM,* which I have outlined, are intended to achieve this double purpose—whether or not one finally thinks they are fully effective. Ecumenists have long since learned that the cause of unity is poorly served by overt denunciations of particular positions, but the clear implication of *BEM* is that some churches have, at times, been quite wrong, and that all churches have been partial and in need of repentance and transformation. Thus, while I can agree with many criticisms of *BEM,* I absolutely disagree with Markus Barth when he contends that "in BEM, we are confronted with nothing better than an accumulation of incompatible beliefs."[9] That comment is based on a particular understanding of the relationship of truth and diversity, one quite foreign to the spirit of *BEM.*

THE RESPONSE TO *BEM*

What are the churches now saying as they respond to this important ecumenical achievement? At the time of this writing, I have not had

9. Barth, "BEM: Questions and Considerations," *Theology Today* 42 (Jan. 1986): 496.

access to many official responses from churches in other parts of the world, but I have surveyed nearly twenty responses from U.S. churches and episcopal conferences, including those of churches from a variety of traditions—Roman Catholic, Orthodox, Lutheran, Anglican, Methodist, Reformed, Baptist, Disciple, and Adventist.[10] While it would be impossible to generalize too freely, I do feel confident in offering the following three observations pertinent to our focus on diversity and truth.

1. There is a widespread willingness to entertain renewal as a result of ecumenical dialogue. Several of the churches devote large portions of their responses to the positive challenges that *BEM* posed for them. Let me give two somewhat surprising examples. The general board of the American Baptist churches states that the baptism section could help its affiliated congregations avoid "an excessive and unbiblical individualization or privatization," while the section on eucharist "offers us the opportunity to deepen our understanding of this 'memorial,' to escape from a very 'thin' notion of 'remembrance.'"[11] A similar tone is found in the "official response" prepared by the Orthodox Theological Society in America. It acknowledges that *BEM*'s warning against indiscriminate baptism and its insistence that churches take more seriously their responsibility for nurturing baptized children to mature commitment in Christ are applicable to Orthodox churches and should be heeded. The Society also noted that the eucharist section in *BEM* can serve as a warning against several tendencies common to Orthodox churches, including "passive worship," "formalism," and "an individualistic approach to the act of Holy Communion."

I regard this as a very positive development. A genuine attempt to be more truly the church God wills means approaching a document like *BEM* as an opportunity for growth rather than an opportunity to belabor the inadequacies of others. While one or two churches give no hint that they may have something to learn from this ecumenically produced text, most indicate an openness to rethink, for the sake of unity and renewal, such difficult issues as rebaptism, frequency of communion, and the ordering of ordained ministry.

10. At the time this was written, one volume of international responses had been published by the WCC: *Churches Respond to BEM,* ed. Max Thurian (Geneva: World Council of Churches, 1986). Since that time three more volumes have appeared. Most of the U.S. church responses on which the following pages are based are included in those volumes, but a few are still available only in manuscript form.

11. *Churches Respond to BEM,* vol. III, ed. Max Thurian (Geneva: World Council of Churches, 1987), pp. 259-60.

2. There seems to be a willingness to accept a widening range of diversity as legitimate. "What Faith and Order wants to destroy," according to one of its vice-moderators, the Roman Catholic theologian Jean M. R. Tillard, "is not diversity but division. In other words, it seeks a *koinonia* in which a strong unity in the essential element of Christian faith makes possible a large diversity in everything deriving from this kernel"[12]—a principle that most responses seem implicitly to endorse.

A good example is the response prepared by the Bishops' Committee for Ecumenical and Interreligious Affairs of the National Conference of Catholic Bishops. Is disagreement over the way Christ's presence is related to the elements an acceptable diversity? Listen to the U.S. Catholic response:

> In the hierarchy of truths, the developed Catholic explanation of the mode [of Christ's presence] is not critically fundamental for acceptance by other Christian traditions in order for them to recognize the faith of the Church through the ages. Thus, the recognition of the real, sacramental presence and of Christ's body and blood truly received agrees with Catholic teaching, although our later dogma univocally states the change of bread and wine into the body and blood.

Equally heartening for Protestant partners is the proposal by the U.S. Bishops' Committee that Rome consider two degrees of recognition of ordained ministry: (a) "real and full ministry" (based on sacramental, episcopal ordination in apostolic succession), and (b) "real but not full apostolic ministry of word, sacrament and service that is fruitful of faith and salvation for its members."

Some readers may find this openness to wider diversity on the part of the Roman Catholic Church surprising, particularly in light of recent attempts by Rome to limit theological expression within its own ranks. However, the U.S. statement is by no means anomalous when set alongside other recent Catholic ecumenical pronouncements. Vatican II's *Decree on Ecumenism* refers approvingly to Acts 15:28: "For it has seemed good to the Holy Spirit and to us to lay upon you no greater burden than these necessary things"—a sentiment echoed by Cardinal Ratzinger when he notes that "maximal demands would wreck the quest for unity."[13] The Lutheran-Roman

12. Tillard, "BEM: The Call for a Judgement upon the Churches and the Ecumenical Movement," *Midstream*, July 1984, p. 238.
13. Ratzinger, "The Future of Ecumenism," *Theology Digest*, Fall 1987, p. 202.

Catholic international dialogue affirms that "unity in Christ does not exist despite and in opposition to diversity, but is given *with and in diversity*. The work of the one unifying Spirit of God does not begin with the uniting of the already separated, but rather creates and maintains diverse realities precisely in order to lead them into the unity of love."[14] And we should not forget the widely discussed work of Rahner and Fries (referred to in Chapter I), who contend that unity is possible now if the churches would (a) commit themselves together to the basic Christian teaching as found in the Bible and the early creeds, and (b) agree not to reject as contrary to the gospel any dogmatic teachings of the other uniting churches.[15]

But if the Rahner-Fries book is indicative of a new willingness to accept doctrinal diversity, the controversy surrounding it indicates that the question "How much consensus is needed on how many issues before greater unity is possible?" is far from being resolved. One response to the work in *L'Osservatore Romano* dismisses the authors' proposals as "absolutely unacceptable" and contends that "reunion" with Rome will require "assent to each and every dogma" professed by the Roman Catholic Church as well as assent to the church's teaching authority as the place where truth is articulated.[16] Such "hardline" statements, though not to be dismissed too lightly, actually serve as reminders of how flexible the official responses really are.

For its part, Faith and Order has never suggested that consensus is necessary on the full range of dogmatic categories. Rather, it has sought convergence only in those areas where the church, because of its lack of common theological understanding, remains visibly divided. Specifically, Faith and Order has talked about three "requirements for visible unity" (requirements echoed by the whole WCC at the Vancouver Assembly):

- a full mutual recognition of our common baptism, eucharist and ministry (not uniformity of liturgical practice or theological expression but a common understanding sufficient for mutual recognition and regular eucharistic sharing)
- common ways of decision making and of teaching the faith authoritatively (not an authoritarian super-church but structures that will enable Christians to take responsibility for one another and to engage in common witness and service)

14. In *Growth in Agreement,* p. 221.

15. Fries and Rahner, *Unity of the Churches: An Actual Possibility,* trans. Ruth and Eric Gritsch (Philadelphia: Fortress Press, 1985).

16. Daniel Ols, "Ecumenical Shortcuts," *L'Osservatore Romano,* 25-26 Feb. 1985, pp. 1, 5.

- a common understanding and expression of the apostolic faith (not credal uniformity but an acknowledgment that our various formulations are grounded in the faith of the Church handed on from the time of the apostles and an ability to confess this faith together, at least on occasion)[17]

3. There is one issue on which Faith and Order did not achieve even modest convergence and over which the responses are also divided: the ordination of women. For purposes of our argument, it is important to note that those churches which favor such ordination are themselves divided into two groups. The Presbyterian Church (U.S.A.), for example, affirms its conviction that "the ordination of women is a faithful expression of the apostolic tradition," and clearly states that it will not back off its own practice of ordaining women for the sake of unity. But its response also contends that this issue "is not an obstacle to our recognition of ordination from churches which do not ordain women."[18] This position is compatible with *BEM,* which suggests that the present impasse need not be a "substantive hindrance" to efforts toward mutual recognition of ministries (M54). This implies that, if recognition is mutual, differences over the question of ordaining women can be regarded as an acceptable diversity. Deeper fellowship is possible without the common claiming of a particular theological understanding and ecclesiastical practice.

The response of the United Church of Christ would seem to represent an alternative perspective. This response quotes a local study committee that asks, "Is it not just as reprehensible to bar a woman from full ministry as it is to bar men because they are black?" This implies that the issue strikes at the very heart of the faith, the denial of women's ordination perhaps constituting a violation of the truth of the Incarnation itself. Just as we do not insist that the eucharistic president be a Palestinian Jew, we dare not insist (at the risk of violating Christ's universality) that that person be male. Thus, concludes the UCC response, "Closer relationships with churches which do not ordain women will undoubtedly be compromised until this matter is resolved."[19] I am quite sure that the United Church of Christ would not argue that the Bulgarian Orthodox Church is not a part of Christ's body or that the Roman Catholic Church has placed itself

17. *Gathered for Life: Official Report, VI Assembly of the World Council of Churches,* ed. David Gill (Geneva: World Council of Churches, 1983), p. 45.
18. *Churches Respond to BEM,* vol. III, p. 200.
19. *Churches Respond to BEM,* vol. II, ed. Max Thurian (Geneva: World Council of Churches, 1986), p. 332.

outside the community of dialogue because it refuses to ordain women to full sacramental ministry. But the UCC does seem to be saying that continued refusal to ordain women is not acceptable in the church God is calling us to become. In the long run, this is not a legitimate diversity.

DOCTRINAL RECONCILIATION: FIVE PROPOSITIONS

This chapter has focused attention on a particular multilateral dialogue aimed at helping churches overcome theological divisions. Before ending this discussion, I would like to make it more general, offering five propositions regarding the search for doctrinal reconciliation in our era. These propositions are drawn from my own experience with ecumenical dialogue around the world, but they are also indebted to the work of Avery Dulles, an American Catholic theologian whose writings constitute, in my opinion, some of the most creative contemporary scholarship on this segment of the ecumenical agenda.

1. The search for doctrinal agreement (which can mean agreement that differences once thought to be divisive need not be so) is an essential part of the ecumenical movement. This may sound obvious, but my experience at the WCC indicates that this proposition is by no means universally held. There are some who dismiss *BEM* as little more than elitist nit-picking over obsolete issues at a time when matters like apartheid and the arms race ought to be claiming the church's attention and resources. Others, including Konrad Raiser, former deputy general secretary of the WCC, accuse Faith and Order of approaching the problem from the wrong direction:

> The division and separation of the churches was the result not of theological differences but of broken fellowship and communion, which was then confirmed by the fact that you no longer had the language to communicate with one another. Finally you perceived the other's affirmations as mutually exclusive of your own and thus as heresy. In the same way, I believe, the unity of the church will not be the product of theological consensus but of growing together in newly discovered fellowship and commitment.[20]

Throughout this book I will argue that doctrinal reconciliation, active engagement for justice, and joyful witness for Christ should not be competing priorities but authentic, complementary responses to

20. Raiser, "A Conversation about 'a Kind of Conversion,'" *One World,* Nov. 1983, p. 16.

the one gospel. The unity for which we work and pray is depicted in Scripture as a community of trust and common service, but also as a community of shared faith and common worship. Indeed, these elements are inseparable: a church's moral teaching, evangelistic witness, and social advocacy necessarily rest on its understanding of God and are sustained by its life of prayer. "The Church," writes Dulles, "cannot be properly understood simply as a coalition for action. It is first of all a community of faith and witness, and as such requires a shared vision."[21] Work such as *BEM* helps clarify that vision, and in so doing it builds trust—which in turn forms the context for further doctrinal convergence. In short, theological dialogue aimed at overcoming doctrinal separation is not an end in itself, nor is it the beginning and end of ecumenism. But, given our present state of ecclesial brokenness, such dialogue is an invaluable means for helping us to be more truly the church God wills.

2. The search for doctrinal agreement, theological conversation on what is "essential" for genuine church unity, needs to take place in the widest possible community of dialogue. This is so central to all that has been said in this book that I need not argue it further here. I do need to add, however, that this proposition does not mean that bilateral conversations (e.g., Lutheran–Roman Catholic) are necessarily inferior to multilateral ones (e.g., the work of Faith and Order in *BEM*). The strength of the two-party dialogues is their capacity to focus on specific areas of tension between churches. They have made a great contribution to the modern search for unity (a contribution that will be further discussed in Chapter V). But the various bilateral discussions can become isolated from one another if they are not deliberately pursued in the context of the whole ecumenical movement.

3. Diversity on matters of doctrine is not only inevitable but desirable. This means that (a) the list of essentials (on which consensus is needed) should be kept as short as possible and (b) the extent of the consensus on each issue should be kept to the minimum needed to insure common faith. The key concept, as I have implied throughout this chapter, is "recognition": Can we recognize in the formulations (and actual practice) of the other church a legitimate expression of the apostolic faith, despite the fact that those formulations vary from our own? The churches have been nourished by different environments; the question is not whether they look the same but whether their roots are in the same soil. The report of the Third

21. Dulles, "Paths to Doctrinal Agreement: Ten Theses," *Theological Studies* 47 (1986): 32.

Forum on Bilateral Conversations puts the point clearly in its discussion of "consensus":

> Consensus is not to be identified with complete unanimity and uniformity of theological understanding. Such is not found within the existing unity of particular churches and should not be expected from dialogue between churches. . . . There is a legitimate necessity for unity in fundamental faith; but there is also an equally necessary freedom in the diversity of its spiritual, liturgical and theological expression. Rather than the demand for cumulative precisions, there should be a basic trust in the dialogue partner's *intentio fidei*.[22]

4. There are already a number of things agreed upon among churches involved in ecumenical dialogue: the Scriptures, the ancient creeds (including their Trinitarian and Christological affirmations), the emerging agreement on the sacraments and ministry. . . . Writes Dulles, "Churches sharing such a wealth of common beliefs, and the kind of worship and practice that flow from them, ought not to regard one another as strangers."[23] The fact that we still do treat one another as strangers (at least to some extent)—refusing to meet around the same table, retreating at critical moments to the autonomy of our decision-making structures—indicates that the lack of ecumenical growth is now due more to a failure of will than to theological difference.

> We have now reached a crucial point in our ecumenical discussions. As we have come to know one another better our eyes have been opened to the depth and pain of our separations and also to our fundamental unity. The measure of unity which it has been given to the churches to experience together must now find clear manifestation.[24]

These powerful words were spoken by Faith and Order not at its 1982 meeting in Lima but thirty years earlier in Lund. How many conferences have been held, how many promising agreements reached, since then! Jürgen Moltmann, reflecting on these achievements, offers a new version of the Lund challenge:

> Now that the doctrinal differences dividing the churches have

22. *Three Reports of the Forum on Bilateral Conversations* (Geneva: World Council of Churches, 1981), p. 18.
23. Dulles, "Paths to Doctrinal Agreement," p. 36.
24. Cited in *A Documentary History of the Faith and Order Movement*, ed. Lukas Vischer (St. Louis: Bethany Press, 1963), p. 86.

been overcome, at least in outline, the theological problems facing us are questions that the churches cannot solve separately, they can only solve them together. They are missionary problems of Christianity throughout the world and the ethical problems facing all Christians in the divided and insecure world we live in today. Time is running out![25]

I repeat a theme of this entire book: Since most churches do share so much already, and since unity and common renewal are so obviously needed for our witness in the world, our basic orientation to each other—the framework of every dialogue—should be one of hopeful openness rather than suspicious protection. Two lines from Hans Küng and Raymond Brown could serve as axioms for contemporary ecumenism. "I have come to the conclusion," writes Küng, "that at this point in history it is the duty of theologians in either camp [Protestant and Catholic] to discover what is worthwhile in the other camp and what is wrong in their own camp."[26] "I contend," writes Brown, "that in a divided Christianity, instead of reading the Bible to assure ourselves that we are right, we would do better to read it to discover where we have not been listening."[27]

5. We have seen that many old divisions may prove to be acceptable diversities when set in new contexts through dialogue. But the purpose of dialogue is not only to show how we can avoid perpetuating divisions based on obsolete disputes; it is also to direct our attention toward areas of needed common renewal as well as errors and idolatries of our day against which we now need—together—to confess. Dulles observes that when today's Catholics or Lutherans or Calvinists look back over lists of propositions condemned by their forebears, these "grievous errors" of an earlier age often sound rather harmless. Part of the reason for this, of course, is that we no longer face the particular situation which provoked the condemnation. "Today we are perhaps in a position," writes Dulles, "to say that the state of emergency—or, in Lutheran terminology, the *status confessionis*—that prompted these declarations has subsided. What is required today is the integral confession of the Christian faith in a manner opposed to the errors to which we ourselves are tempted."[28]

25. Moltmann, "What Kind of Unity?" in *Lausanne 77* (Geneva: World Council of Churches, 1977), p. 40.
26. Küng, in *Steps to Christian Unity*, ed. John A. O'Brien (Garden City, N.Y.: Doubleday, 1964), p. 77.
27. Brown, *The Churches the Apostles Left Behind* (New York: Paulist Press, 1984), p. 150.
28. Dulles, "Paths to Doctrinal Agreement," p. 40.

We now see, more clearly than in the past, that one of the errors to which we are always tempted is that of absolutizing our relative perspectives. This should make us very wary of dismissing the witness of others who claim the name of Christ. But it should also make us aware of the need to renew constantly our understandings and practices in order that they bear more faithful witness to the sovereignty of God and the lordship of Christ.

Baptism and eucharist can serve as examples of what I have in mind. In my opinion, the most agonizing question with regard to the latter is that posed by the Sri Lankan Catholic theologian Tissa Balasuriya. In his book entitled *The Eucharist and Human Liberation,* Balasuriya asks how it is possible "that societies calling themselves Christian can offer the Eucharist weekly, for years, without improving the relationships among persons in it. . . . Why is it that in spite of hundreds of thousands of eucharistic celebrations, Christians continue as selfish as before?"[29]

After centuries of hostility and division over questions of "real presence," "memorial," and "sacrifice," churches involved in ecumenical conversations are now able to say, "Many of these disputes can be put behind us." And thus we are in a position to address together through dialogue the kinds of questions Balasuriya poses.

The same is true with regard to baptism. "Isn't it strange," asks Walter Brueggemann, "that in our union conversations, we make a great deal over the differences of adult and infant baptism, of immersion or sprinkling? But the real issue is that, because we are baptized, we discern the world differently."[30] Shouldn't dialogue help us acknowledge that in baptism, at whatever age it is administered, the church distinguishes itself from the world? Shouldn't dialogue help us acknowledge more forcefully than we have that Christ's claim on the one baptized is greater than *all* other claims and that this makes a significant difference in the way one thinks about and deals with war or the distribution of the world's resources? *BEM* is far from irrelevant if it enables us to "clear the decks" for the truly relevant questions of our day, if it moves beyond the negotiating of past disputes to a creative common envisioning of what we are called to be as followers of Christ.

29. Balasuriya, *The Eucharist and Human Liberation* (Maryknoll, N.Y.: Orbis Books, 1979), pp. 21, xi.

30. From a manuscript copy of an address delivered to the 1985 General Assembly of the Christian Church (Disciples of Christ).

CHAPTER IV

SOCIAL DIVERSITY: IS THE JUSTIFICATION OF APARTHEID AN ACCEPTABLE DIVERSITY?

Is apartheid a heresy? Can denominations that support this ideology of racial separation, either through their theology or through their practice, be considered part of the true church of Jesus Christ? How should the worldwide church respond to the present situation in South Africa and to those "churches" identified with the white-run status quo?

Such questions (which will be the focus of this chapter) indicate why this topic is both the easiest and the most difficult one with which we will deal. On the one hand, the international condemnation of the Afrikaner churches constitutes the most celebrated case in our era of drawing lines between church and pseudo-church. Indeed, it is arguably the only contemporary case of general ecumenical consensus on the limits of diversity. On the other hand, if we expand the question only slightly, it is clear that diversity on social issues is the most emotionally charged, divisive topic facing the church.

This last point was forcefully made by José Miguez Bonino in an influential address to a 1973 Faith and Order consultation in Salamanca. In Latin America, Miguez Bonino argued, denominational differences are often smoke screens that obscure real divisions. Sacraments and ministry are discussed irenically, while the polemics are reserved for conflicting definitions of what it means to be the church in mission in the world. Tempers flare and Christians part company over the way in which the church relates to the struggle for a new social and political order. It is not possible to be the church in today's world, Miguez Bonino contended, without declaring a position in this struggle (not to choose in a situation of oppression is to choose for the status quo). And it is not possible to speak of unity or authentic community apart from the new patterns

58

of division and convergence that emerge in light of this quest for a new kind of human life in a new society.[1]

There is a strong tendency in the contemporary church for defenders of a particular social-political position to assume that openness to much diversity only weakens the church's ability to combat the evil they oppose (just as radicals such as Herbert Marcuse attacked theories of social tolerance in the 1960s), and a concomitant tendency to emphasize particular truth claims at the expense of real dialogue with alternative perspectives. This leads to a familiar polarization in which those who refuse to support the African National Congress (or similar organizations) are characterized as reactionary defenders of racism (i.e., as hardly Christian), while those who support social revolution in South Africa (or elsewhere) are denounced as communist sympathizers (i.e., as hardly Christian). The tension between truth and diverse community is, in either case, severely tested.

In this chapter I want to examine what the ecumenical movement has said and done about racism, and especially about the church struggle in South Africa. Are there lessons to be learned from recent attempts (e.g., by the WCC and the World Alliance of Reformed Churches) to impose definite limits on diversity? In light of this discussion I will conclude the chapter with four observations regarding the future of the ecumenical movement.

RACISM AND THE ECUMENICAL MOVEMENT

Since its beginnings the modern ecumenical movement has opposed racism and shown support for the victims of it. One of the patriarchs of modern ecumenism, J. H. Oldham, offered an early statement with the book he published in 1924 entitled *Christianity and the Race Problem*. Racism, the use of a person's racial origins to determine her or his value, was explicitly condemned by the Oxford conference on Life and Work in 1937 and by the Amsterdam Assembly of the WCC in 1948—though both meetings were, for obvious reasons, more directly concerned with anti-Semitism, and both spoke of racism as a problem of mission (i.e., racial segregation and oppression undermine the church's witness) rather than as an ecclesiological issue (i.e., racial inclusiveness is a fundamental mark of the church and its unity).

However, there was another episode that placed the ecclesiologi-

1. Miguez Bonino, "A Latin American Attempt to Locate the Question of Unity," in *What Kind of Unity?* (Geneva: World Council of Churches, 1974), pp. 51ff.

cal question before the churches in the ecumenical movement in a
most dramatic way: namely, the German Church Struggle of the
1930s, and especially the famous Barmen Declaration of 1934.
Since Barmen is frequently appealed to as a precedent for the contemporary battle with apartheid, it deserves more than passing mention.

The Barmen Declaration was a response made by the first synod
of the German Confessing Church to the "German Christians," the
dominant state-supported movement within German Christianity that
welcomed the leadership of Adolf Hitler and the ideology of Nazism.
"Guiding Principles" for the German Christian movement, published
in June of 1932, called for a union of German evangelical churches
around the understanding that "race, folk and nation [are] orders of
existence granted and entrusted to us by God. God's law for us is that
we look to the preservation of these orders." It was claimed that the
"Principles" were based on faith in Christ, a "heroic piety," and the
spirit of Luther. They denounced Marxism, the Center Party, inter-
marriage between Jews and Aryan Germans, and any mission to the
Jews. What we want, said the leaders of this movement, is "an evangelical Church that is rooted in our nationhood. We repudiate the
spirit of a Christian world-citizenship." The church must be "in the
forefront of the crucial battle for the existence of our people." In the
present church "we miss a confident daring for God and for the mission of the Church. The way into the Kingdom of God is through
struggle, cross, and sacrifice, not through a false peace."[2] (This language reminds one of both sides of various contemporary debates.)

One further example may serve to indicate even more precisely
what the Barmen Declaration opposed. In November of 1933, six
months before the Barmen Synod, a mass meeting of the German
Christian movement in the Berlin Sports Palace heard an explicit call
for a new, mighty, and united German Reich Church. That gathering
of twenty thousand also passed—with but one dissenting vote—a resolution calling for the following:

- the discharge of ministers unwilling to cooperate with National
  Socialism
- the removal of all Christians with "alien blood" to a Jewish Christian church
- the removal of anything "un-Germanic" from the church service
  and confession (including the Old Testament)

2. Arthur C. Cochrane, *The Church's Confession under Hitler* (Philadelphia: Westminster Press, 1962), pp. 222-23.

- the freeing of the gospel from its "Oriental distortions"
- the reformulation of the idea of service (diakonia) as service to fellow Aryans.[3]

Barmen resoundingly rejected such assertions. The first of its six propositions is the linchpin: "Jesus Christ, as he is attested to us in Holy Scripture, is the one Word of God which we have to hear and which we have to trust and obey in life and in death." It goes on to denounce as "false doctrine" the idea that other events, powers, figures, or "truths" can be the source of the church's proclamation. In other words, the Barmen Synod sought to confess the Christian faith in a public and authoritative way even though its delegates knew that such confession would be divisive. In fact, that was the point. Where these "destructive errors" of the German Christians obtain, said Barmen, "the church . . . ceases to be the church."[4] Christians should not be fooled by talk of unity in Christ and the mission of the church. The German Christian program, in its absorption of Nazi ideology as an alternative source of revelation, had gone beyond the limits of acceptable unity and diversity.

All of this is shown in even sharper relief in the writings of Karl Barth (the major author of the Barmen Declaration) from this period. For example, in his thunderous reply to what were called the Rengsdorf Theses, Barth contended that "whoever preaches today 'a Christianity rooted in German nationality' binds God's Word to an arbitrarily conceived Weltanschauung, thereby invalidating it, and places himself outside the evangelical Church." The theology behind the German Christian movement, Barth concluded, was "to be entirely rejected and opposed just for the sake of Christian love."[5]

The German Church Struggle made a decisive impact on the young ecumenical movement because it confronted that movement with the need to choose between two antithetical confessions. It is clear that various ecumenical leaders, such as Willem Visser 't Hooft, gave strong and consistent support to the Confessing Church. The only major conference to do so, however, was the 1934 Fan meeting of Life and Work. Dietrich Bonhoeffer was among those who saw the Fan participants' willingness to discuss the concept and actuality of heresy as a great step forward for ecumenical Christianity, but the truth was that "at Fan the ecumenical movement had gone as far as it

---

3. Cochrane, The Church's Confession under Hitler, p. 112.

4. The Barmen Declaration is widely reprinted; see, for example, John Leith's Creeds of the Churches (Atlanta: John Knox Press, 1963), pp. 517-21.

5. Barth, quoted by Cochrane in The Church's Confession under Hitler, pp. 120, 122.

was ever to go in its commitment towards the Confessing Church."[6] The evil had been identified, but concerted action against it proved impossible. Many hoped that the formation of the WCC would correct just this problem.

In the early years of the Council, African churches played little role because, in most African countries, the churches were still not autonomous. The exception was South Africa, which had five constituting members of the WCC, including two Dutch Reformed, Afrikaans-speaking churches that supported the government philosophy of apartheid. Still, at the first full session of the Council's Central Committee held in 1949, the question was raised, mainly by black church leaders from the United States, whether action should be taken concerning the racial situation in South Africa. The idea of sending a multiracial delegation to the country was rejected by the South Africans, but Visser 't Hooft did spend five weeks there in 1952, meeting with church leaders on all sides of the issue. "The important thing," he wrote in his report of the trip, "is to manifest to a world in which the races live in tension, that in Christ their tension is overcome."[7] But he also concluded that dialogue was still possible within the fellowship of the Council.

A similar approach was taken, after much heated debate, at the WCC's Second Assembly, held in Evanston in 1954. A resolution was passed calling on the churches to renounce all forms of segregation and discrimination as contrary to the gospel, and to work for their elimination in the life of their societies. But Visser 't Hooft and others were concerned to keep the Afrikaner churches in the WCC for purposes of dialogue, and so they insisted on adding a qualifying statement recognizing that, for some churches, the immediate achievement of this goal was extremely difficult. One purpose of ecumenical fellowship was to give these churches strength and encouragement to overcome these difficulties. The Dutch Reformed delegates did not vote against the resolution and urged study of it back in South Africa.

The World Council's position began to take a dramatic turn only after the 1960 riots in Sharpeville, during which a number of blacks were killed and following which a state of emergency was declared. The WCC urged a multiracial conference aimed at thorough discus-

6. Eberhard Bethge, *Dietrich Bonhoeffer* (New York: Harper & Row, 1977), p. 309.

7. Visser 't Hooft, *Memoirs* (London: SCM Press, 1973), p. 282. Chapter 34 of this book provides a fascinating perspective on this history of the WCC opposition to apartheid.

sion of apartheid by South African churches, and such a meeting was held at the Cottesloe College Residence of the University of Witwatersrand (Johannesburg) in December of 1961.

The Cottesloe Consultation was a remarkable event. Visser 't Hooft's *Memoirs* indicates that "the sharp lines of demarcation between the various delegations became less pronounced" as a result of the dialogue and common worship.[8] The final report notes that participants held widely divergent convictions on apartheid, but they were still able to agree (with at least an 80 percent majority) on seventeen propositions, including the following:

> No one who believes in Jesus Christ may be excluded from any church on the grounds of his colour or race. The spiritual unity among all men who are in Christ must find visible expression in acts of common worship and witness, and in fellowship and consultation on matters of common concern.

> It is our conviction that the right to own land wherever he is domiciled, and to partake in the government of his country, is part of the dignity of the adult man, and for this reason a policy which permanently denies to non-white people the right of collaboration in the government of the country of which they are citizens cannot be justified.[9]

Naturally, the report was condemned by the South African government as a case of outside meddling. The voices of conciliation within the churches were also shouted down, and both Dutch Reformed bodies withdrew from the WCC.

There were other developments in the World Council itself. The New Delhi Assembly in 1961 established the Secretariat on Racial and Ethnic Relations, but there was a growing sense that the ecumenical penchant for verbal dialogue was not sufficiently matched by committed action. A 1964 consultation in Zambia heard the first talk of the possible need for violence in the face of the deteriorating situation in South Africa. The WCC issued several statements on violence over the next decade, generally upholding nonviolence, but also arguing that racism is itself a form of systemic violence, and that it is dangerous for white, North Atlantic Christians to pass judgment on those caught in the immediate struggle.

A further step was taken when the 1968 Uppsala Assembly of

8. Visser 't Hooft, *Memoirs*, p. 285.
9. "The Cottesloe Consultation Statement, 1961," cited in *Apartheid Is a Heresy*, ed. John W. de Gruchy and Charles Villa-Vicencio (Grand Rapids: Eerdmans, 1983), pp. 150-51.

the WCC called on the churches "to embark on a vigorous campaign against racism." A subsequent meeting, held in Notting Hill in 1969, reaffirmed the right to resist tyranny (i.e., "just revolution") and urged the WCC itself to be involved in the struggle against racism. All else failing, "the Church and churches should support resistance movements, including revolutions, which are aimed at the elimination of political or economic tyranny which makes racism possible."[10]

The same period saw the establishment of the WCC's most controversial department, the Program to Combat Racism, which, according to its bylaws, is "responsible for working out World Council policies and programs combating racism, giving expression to solidarity with the racially oppressed, organizing action-oriented research projects, assisting the churches in the education of their own members for racial justice, and the operation of the Special Fund to Combat Racism." The emphasis had clearly shifted from aiding the victims of racism and providing opportunities for negotiation to supporting those involved in direct confrontation with racism—especially in South Africa, which remained the priority concern.

Another dimension was also being added to the ecumenical discussions: the WCC increasingly spoke of the church as a racially inclusive community. Of course, this had been implicit in the Council's earlier work, but it now emerged as a central theme of ecumenical life. Racism was now seen not simply as an ethical or missionary concern but as a deeply ecclesiological one, as crucial to the struggle for authentic unity as overcoming falsely divisive conceptions of sacraments and ministry. A 1980 WCC consultation on racism said it most directly:

> The Church is called upon to witness to this unity in the midst of cultural differences as a fellowship in Christ gathered from all peoples and cultures. It is meant to be a sign of the reconciled humanity. But our experience shows that denominationalism and racism have destroyed the unity of the Church. Hitherto we have been preoccupied with the disunity arising from denominational divisions. We now realize that the sin of racism contradicts the nature of the Church and its oneness which we confess. . . . Thus combating racism is a significant contribution to the search for both the unity of the Church and humankind.[11]

10. Leon Howell, *Acting in Faith: The World Council of Churches since 1975* (Geneva: World Council of Churches, 1982), p. 78.

11. Barbara Rogers, *Race: No Peace without Justice* (Geneva: World Council of Churches, 1980), p. 120.

OTTAWA AND "KAIROS"

Since the World Council is nothing other than a fellowship of churches, it is not surprising that statements and actions by churches and church families were moving in the same direction as those of the Council. In 1977 the Lutheran World Federation (LWF) called the situation in southern Africa a *status confessionis:* "This means that, on the basis of faith and in order to manifest the unity of the Church, Churches would publicly and unequivocally reject the existing apartheid system."[12] In 1984 the LWF took the further step of suspending the membership of two white, apartheid-supporting Lutheran churches in South Africa and Namibia, arguing that they had already "in fact withdrawn from the confessional community which forms the basis of membership in the Lutheran World Federation."[13] The limits of diversity in Christian fellowship are not determined by the pigmentation of a person's skin; any church that acts as if this is so (e.g., by excluding black people from Holy Communion) has placed itself outside the community of dialogue.

The LWF action is only one example of the current effort to define the limits of acceptable diversity on this issue. Two other documents of recent years deserve close inspection.

First is the resolution on racism and South Africa passed by the World Alliance of Reformed Churches (WARC) at its 1982 General Council in Ottawa, Canada. In their book entitled *Apartheid Is a Heresy,* John de Gruchy and Charles Villa-Vicencio call this decision "the most significant ecclesiastical event affecting the churches in South Africa since the Cottesloe Consultation."[14] Already in 1970 the WARC had called on its members (Reformed, Presbyterian, and Congregationalist churches around the world) "to recognize racism for the idolatry it, in fact, is." "The Church of Jesus Christ," it argued, "does not make room for walls, be they tribal, racial, cultural, economic, national or confessional. The Church that by doctrine and/or practice affirms segregation of peoples (e.g., racial segregation) as a law for its life cannot be regarded as an authentic member of the body of Christ."[15] Two white, Dutch Reformed denomina-

---

12. "Southern Africa: Confessional Integrity," 1977 LWF statement, cited in *Apartheid Is a Heresy,* p. 161. Many of the important church statements are found in the appendices to this volume.

13. See the *Lutheran World Federation Report,* nos. 19-20 (1985), pp. 1-115.

14. *Apartheid Is a Heresy,* p. xv.

15. Nairobi 1970, *Proceedings,* quoted by John de Gruchy in "Towards a Confessing Church," in *Apartheid Is a Heresy,* p. 86.

tions—the Nederduitse Gereformeerde Kerk (NGK) and the smaller Nederduitse Hervormde Kerk—were mentioned by name in the 1970 statement.

In 1982 the Alliance took the next logical step, issuing the statement entitled "Racism and South Africa." The following lines from that document have been among the most widely discussed in the recent history of the church:

> In certain situations the confession of a Church needs to draw a clear line between truth and error. In faithful allegiance to Jesus Christ it may have to reject the claims of an unjust or oppressive government and denounce Christians who aid and abet the oppressor. We believe that this is the situation in South Africa today. . . .
>
> Therefore, the General Council declares that this situation constitutes a *status confessionis* for our Churches, which means that we regard this as an issue on which it is not possible to differ without seriously jeopardizing the integrity of our common confession as Reformed Churches.
>
> We declare with black Reformed Christians of South Africa that apartheid ("separate development") is a sin, and that the moral and theological justification of it is a travesty of the Gospel and, in its persistent disobedience to the Word of God, a theological heresy.[16]

The WARC then suspended the membership of the two churches previously named. This action was of particular significance because of the influential position that the NGK occupies in South African society. Indeed, there is considerable evidence that apartheid was originally a conception of the Afrikaner churches, especially the NGK. In 1948 an NGK publication proudly asserted that "as a Church, we have always worked purposefully for the separation of the races. In this regard apartheid can rightfully be called a Church policy."[17]

The second document I want to examine was written by a multiracial, ecumenical "working committee" in South Africa and published in 1985. It is commonly known as "the Kairos Document" because of its authors' conviction that now is the *kairos* or "moment of truth" for the church and society in South Africa. Two points made throughout this remarkable text bear directly on our topic.

---

16. "Racism and South Africa," 1982 WARC statement, cited in *Apartheid Is a Heresy*, p. 170.

17. Statement quoted by Allan Boesak in "He made us all, but . . . ," in *Apartheid Is a Heresy*, p. 6.

First, the present crisis calls into question traditional understandings of Christian unity. "Both oppressor and oppressed claim loyalty to the same Church. They are both baptised in the same baptism and participate together in the breaking of the same bread, the same body and blood of Christ."[18] Yet it is clear that the churches are fundamentally divided, not along confessional lines but along racial ones. Within the same denomination are people who support and benefit from apartheid, people who oppose and suffer under it, and "some who are trying to sit on the fence." This, says the Kairos Document, is division of the most profound sort, and it demands decision. "There is only one way forward to Church unity and that is for those Christians who find themselves on the side of the oppressor or sitting on the fence, to cross over to the other side to be united in faith and action with those who are oppressed."[19] Unity can only be unity with God, who, according to Psalm 103, "is always on the side of the oppressed." Anything else would be no more than structural merger, masking the real divisions between South African Christians. "As disciples of Jesus we should rather promote truth and justice and life at all costs, even at the cost of creating conflict, disunity and dissension along the way."[20] Truth claims here override the maintenance of diverse community, but that is so because the wrong diversity has been maintained. It is precisely because the church is, by definition (i.e., according to the gospel), a racially diverse community that diversity on the question of apartheid is unacceptable.

The second point made by the Kairos Document that bears on our discussion is this: the present crisis also points to the limits of dialogue. "Kairos" rejects "state theology," that which justifies the racist status quo, as "heretical" and "blasphemous." But much of its critique is aimed at "church theology," that which criticizes apartheid "in a limited, guarded and cautious way." Church theology urges "reconciliation" between the various parties. It says that "we must listen to both sides of the story. If the two sides can only meet to talk and negotiate they will sort out their differences and misunderstandings, and the conflict will be resolved."[21] The Kairos authors firmly disagree, at least with regard to the present situation in South Africa:

> There are conflicts that can only be described as the struggle
> between justice and injustice, good and evil, God and the

18. *The Kairos Document: Challenge to the Church*, rev. 2nd ed. (Grand Rapids: Eerdmans, 1986), p. 2.
19. *The Kairos Document*, p. 28.
20. *The Kairos Document*, p. 11.
21. *The Kairos Document*, p. 9-10.

devil. To speak of reconciling these two is not only a mistaken application of the Christian idea of reconciliation, it is a total betrayal of all that Christian faith has ever meant. Nowhere in the Bible or in Christian tradition has it ever been suggested that we ought to try to reconcile good and evil, God and the devil. We are supposed to do away with evil, injustice, oppression and sin—not come to terms with it. We are supposed to oppose, confront and reject the devil and not try to sup with the devil.[22]

We long for genuine peace, the Kairos authors write, but "the peace that the world [and "church theology"] offers us is a unity that compromises the truth, covers over injustice and oppression and is totally motivated by selfishness."[23] In other words, the current conflict is so unambiguous, so irreconcilable, that dialogue is an inappropriate tool.

It must be added that Anglican Bishop Desmond Tutu, winner of the Nobel peace prize and apartheid's best-known critic, did not sign the Kairos Document. One reason is that the document, in Tutu's opinion, tends to caricature the work of those church leaders who have waged effective battle against the system over the past generation. Another reason is that the bishop refuses "to give up on Pharaoh" altogether, arguing that the gospel demands witness to reconciliation, even at the cost of death. Paul Santmire has written that in the Kairos Document and Tutu's response to it we see extreme but complementary approaches to the current crisis—"one that revives a theology of political resistance and, as a last resort, tyrannicide, and another that revives a theology of bold witness and, as a last resort, martyrdom."[24] Both are authentically Christian, rooted in the Scripture and Tradition of the church.

What can these two texts—the WARC resolution and the Kairos Document—teach us about determining limits of acceptable diversity? Out of the many possible "lessons," I wish to lift up the seven that follow.

1. Most Christians and their churches, I suspect, are guilty of failing to do all they can or should to combat an evil such as apartheid, but the charge of "heresy" is properly reserved for those *churches* that provide theological apology for the evil. There are at least two possible objections to this statement. Some will object that ecumenical churches need to exercise greater discipline over their members.

---

22. *The Kairos Document*, p. 10.
23. *The Kairos Document*, p. 11.
24. Santmire, "The Pathos of South African Theology," *Christian Century*, 30 Oct. 1985, p. 965.

But, even if this is true, there is broad consensus that the fundamental issue is the erring church, not individual heresy. The church will always be a field with tares as well as wheat, but it must be the true field. Others will object that formal confession means little unless backed by faithful acts. At the Uppsala Assembly, Visser 't Hooft warned that those churches which "deny in fact their responsibility for the needy in any part of the world are just as much guilty of heresy as those who deny this or that article of the faith."[25] The English-speaking churches in South Africa are frequently criticized for doing too little to undermine the racist structure, despite their theological opposition to it. Still, no one has suggested that these churches have placed themselves outside the community of dialogue. The denial of truth in practice is presumably a matter of education and recommitment; the denial of truth theologically demands a different type of response.

2. The exclusion of Afrikaner churches from the circle of international Christian fellowship has come as a last resort and, as this chapter has tried to show, on the basis of broad consensus. Roman Catholic bishops in South Africa denounced apartheid as "intrinsically evil" as far back as 1957. But firm lines separating the church from the pseudo-church have been drawn only after exhaustive discussion and prayer involving the universal Christian community (i.e., the broadest "community of interpreters"). The Kairos Document ends by calling upon Christian brothers and sisters around the world to lend their support, but in fact this statement was possible, in part, because the ecumenical church had already spoken loudly and clearly.

3. Any lines drawn between Christians should not be considered permanent. Both the WARC and the LWF have refused to close the door on eventual reconciliation. The WARC, for example, has said that its South African Dutch Reformed members are suspended until (a) black Christians are no longer excluded from church services (especially Holy Communion), (b) concrete support in word and deed is given to those who suffer under apartheid, and (c) synod resolutions are passed that reject apartheid and commit the churches to dismantling it in both church and state. Division is the exception, not the rule. The focus is not on excluding people but on excluding error. The real point is not to draw negative boundaries but to make positive proclamation of the gospel.

4. Lines separating truth from error can be drawn only in a spirit of general repentance. Even if there is ecumenical consensus that

25. Visser 't Hooft, "The Mandate of the Ecumenical Movement," in *The Uppsala Report* (Geneva: World Council of Churches, 1968), p. 320.

one position is right and another wrong, it is certain that neither has been fully faithful to God's will. "Even as we say these things," wrote the Ottawa delegates following their denunciation of apartheid, "we . . . confess that we are not without guilt in regard to racism. Racism is a reality everywhere and its existence calls for repentance and concerted action."[26]

5. The direction of movement is important. If a church is becoming increasingly discriminatory, or if it shows little positive movement despite repeated appeals (as was the case in both the WARC and the LWF), then fellowship may need to be broken. If, however, an erring church shows movement toward greater inclusivity, then the proper response would seem to be encouragement and further challenge.

6. It is important to acknowledge that there are points beyond which dialogue is no longer possible if truth is to be served, but even the Kairos Document admits that "there is no specifically Christian solution," no single political strategy that must be followed by faithful churches and their members.[27] Even if there is no room for dialogue on the fundamental issue—for example, that apartheid is a denial of the gospel and must be actively opposed in the name of Christ—dialogue remains appropriate, even necessary, with regard to the question of *how* it should be opposed.

7. The struggle against apartheid indicates that it is impossible to maintain the distinction between "social" and "theological" issues. It is painfully true, writes John de Gruchy, professor of religious studies at the University of Capetown, that we have inherited the confessional divisions of Europe. But, he adds,

> it is equally true, and more painful, that these confessional divisions have been exacerbated by separation along racial, cultural and ethnic lines. These issues, normally regarded as nontheological, must now be seen as equally confessional, because they have to do with the truth of the Gospel as much as those that, for example, traditionally separate Catholics from Calvinists.[28]

WARNINGS AND CHALLENGES

Thus far I have tried to lift up conclusions drawn from particular

---

26. "Racism and South Africa," 1982 WARC statement, cited in *Apartheid Is a Heresy,* p. 172.

27. *The Kairos Document,* p. 15.

28. De Gruchy, "Towards a Confessing Church," in *Apartheid Is a Heresy,* p. 80.

documents related to the ecumenical discussion of apartheid. In the final section of this chapter I wish to range more broadly, offering four observations on the future of the ecumenical movement stemming, in a general way, from these discussions of social diversity. The last chapter ended with propositions related to the traditional agenda of Faith and Order. Here I want to suggest a list of "warnings" and "challenges" more closely allied to the traditional agenda of Life and Work. Once again, however, the focus of attention is on the tension between truth and diverse community.

1. It is apparent that the contention of Miguez Bonino with which we began this chapter is correct: the lines of division or potential division have shifted in our century and, more especially, in our generation. Lines are still drawn (and need to be drawn), but not necessarily where previous generations have drawn them. As Dietrich Bonhoeffer once wrote,

> The knowledge of the extent of the Church is never theoretically at the Church's disposal but must always be ascertained at any given moment. . . . This brings the element of living decision into the determination of the boundaries of the Church. The boundaries of the Church are always decided only in the encounter between the Church and unbelief; the act is a decision of the Church.[29]

And this means, of course, that the real lines of contemporary division which the church needs to confront are not necessarily (or even usually) addressed in dialogues between churches based on identities inherited from the past.

2. More attention needs to be given in the ecumenical movement to helping the churches distinguish between ethical norms, derived generally from Scripture, and specific policy applications of such normative principles. Biblical norms (e.g., the obligation of Christians to seek justice for the poor) properly help define the nature and limits of Christian fellowship. Policy decisions (e.g., the determination that the Sandinista revolution is an appropriate expression of justice for the poor and therefore deserves the support of Christians) will evoke strong convictions—in fact, it seems to be a law of human nature that the more concrete the issue, the stronger the conviction—but these should *not* be the cause of division or continuing separation.

Churches have a right—even an obligation, in my opinion—to speak out through their decision-making processes on significant

29. Bonhoeffer, quoted by de Gruchy in "Towards a Confessing Church," in *Apartheid Is a Heresy*, p. 79.

questions of political and social policy. But it must be remembered that their policy decisions, though backed by the authority of ecclesial decision-making bodies, are the transient products of particular historical moments. Differences over policy decisions (e.g., support for the African National Congress in the struggle against apartheid) should be shared *within* the fellowship of those who confess Jesus Christ.

In light of all that, the real issue becomes "How specific should we make our basic norms?" Should we insist on justice? Justice for the poor? Justice for the poor through political struggle? There is no way I can answer such questions in this volume; but it may be useful to identify what are sometimes called "middle axioms." A middle axiom, to borrow a definition from Gabriel Fackre, "is one which does not specify the concrete application of the principle to a person, party, or program, but does scale down the more abstract norms to the ethos in which specific judgments are to be made."[30] (Support for the poor in Latin America in their current struggles to be freed from economic exploitation might be an example of a middle axiom.) This kind of "scaling down" is an interpretive task and, like other interpretive tasks, should be undertaken in the broadest possible community. A church should expect real debate during the process, but, as with policy decisions, it should be possible to disagree over middle axioms and still be common members of one community.

In my opinion, the best recent example of responsible distinguishing between ethical norms and specific policies or middle axioms is the National Conference of Catholic Bishops' pastoral letter on war and peace, *The Challenge of Peace: God's Promise and Our Response*. The bishops begin by stating "principles, norms and premises of Catholic teaching," including the following unequivocal declaration: "Peacemaking is not an optional commitment. It is a requirement of our faith. We are called to be peacemakers, not by some movement of the moment, but by our Lord Jesus."[31] They also make it clear, however, that not all parts of the pastoral letter carry such weight:

> We wish to explore and explain the resources of the moral-religious teaching and to apply it to specific questions of the day. . . . At times we state universally binding moral prin-

30. Fackre, *The Religious Right and Christian Faith* (Grand Rapids: Eerdmans, 1982), p. 78.

31. National Conference of Catholic Bishops, *The Challenge of Peace: God's Promise and Our Response* (United States Catholic Conference, 1983), p. vii.

ciples found in the teaching of the Church; at other times the pastoral letter makes specific applications, observations and recommendations which allow for diversity of opinion on the part of those who assess the factual data of situations differently.[32]

According to the pastoral letter, examples of middle axioms or policy applications on which diversity is acceptable include the following:

- *Support for pacifism or the "just war" theory*
  They diverge on some specific conclusions, but they share a common presumption against the use of force as a means of settling disputes. (p. 37)

- *Acceptance of policies of nuclear deterrence*
  Although reasons exist which move some to condemn reliance on nuclear weapons for deterrence, we have not reached this conclusion for the reasons outlined in this letter. (p. 61)

- *Support for the possibility of nuclear retaliation to conventional attack*
  Our conclusions and judgments in this area although based on careful study and reflection of the application of moral principles do not have, of course, the same force as the principles themselves and therefore allow for different opinions. (p. 48)

- *The decision of whether or not to work for the U.S. defense industry*
  We recognize the possibility of diverse concrete judgments being made in this complex area. (p. 95)

3. At present, apartheid is the only situation on which the international church has spoken in concert of *status confessionis,* but this may well change in the next generation, just as a consensus that apartheid is a sin and its theological justification a heresy has emerged through ecumenical dialogue in the present generation. Already some churches (e.g., the Reformed Church in Germany) have argued that support for policies of nuclear deterrence constitutes a threat to creation itself, a threat so grave that diversity on the issue should not be tolerated in authoritative church pronouncements. That

32. *The Challenge of Peace,* p. i.

is to say, the gospel calls us to go beyond the bishops' pastoral, restricting the range of acceptable Christian diversity even at the risk of division. As I noted in Chapter I, the WCC declared at its last assembly that "the nuclear weapons issue [by which it means both the possession and the use of nuclear weapons] is, in its import and threat to humanity, a question of Christian discipline and faithfulness to the Gospel."[33] It seems likely that the Council will soon call on its members to make a mutual commitment to "justice, peace and the integrity of creation"—which would demand far more than rhetoric. Even more problematic would be recognition of the world economic system as a situation demanding a confession of faith. This, too, has been debated in World Council circles.[34]

4. I come back, finally, to the point I made at the end of the last chapter: opposition to an evil such as apartheid and reconciliation of divisions within the church (such as different theologies and practices of baptism) are intertwined elements of the same agenda. For one thing, apartheid is a *doctrinal* concern. It denies the truth that all humans are created in the image of God, denies that the liberating work of Christ extends equally to those of all races and classes, and thereby undermines the baptismal unity of Christ's body. For another, barriers in church and society often reflect the same fear of that which is strange, foreign, unlike ourselves. Xenophobia is dangerous both to racial minorities and to the ecumenical community; openness to human diversity as an avenue to truth and wholeness is the food on which both are nourished.

33. *Gathered for Life: Official Report, VI Assembly of the World Council of Churches,* ed. David Gill (Geneva: World Council of Churches, 1983), p. 137.
34. See Ulrich Duchrow, *Global Economy: A Confessional Issue for the Churches?* trans. David Lewis (Geneva: World Council of Churches, 1987).

CHAPTER V

CONFESSIONAL DIVERSITY: IS DENOMINATIONAL IDENTITY AN ACCEPTABLE DIVERSITY?

Having looked at the way the ecumenical movement is determining what is and is not acceptable diversity on such issues as the sacraments and racial inclusivity, I want to turn now to what is, in some ways, an even thornier question: Is "confessional identity" (Lutheran, Presbyterian, Roman Catholic, and so on) an acceptable diversity? In the future unity that we envision, is there room not just for the riches of the various confessional traditions but for their continuation in some recognizable form? We will begin with a discussion of the goal of church unity, especially as it has been expressed in the ecumenical movement over the past twenty-five years, and then go on to examine the arguments of those who favor and reject confessional identity as part of future unity. I will conclude the chapter by putting myself on the line with eight observations.

CONCEPTS AND MODELS OF UNITY

Concepts of unity are not, of course, the invention of modern ecumenism. The churches brought with them into the ecumenical movement various notions of what unity would require. Lukas Vischer, former director of the Faith and Order Commission, has suggested five such conceptualizations, a list that provides a useful framework for beginning our discussion.[1]

1. Some churches, and many individual Christians, have insisted that unity is primarily or solely a matter of spiritual harmony. The classic statement of this position is probably that of John Wesley: "I

1. Vischer, "Drawn and Held Together by the Reconciling Power of Christ," *Ecumenical Review* 26 (Apr. 1974): 172-73.

ask not, therefore, of him with whom I would unite in love . . . do you receive the supper of the Lord in the same posture and manner that I do? nor whether, in the administration of baptism you agree with me. . . . My only question is this, 'Is thine heart right, as my heart is with thy heart?'" Such a spiritual bond seeks external expression, but the forms of fellowship are considered secondary and in need of constant re-creation. The ecumenical movement has generally agreed that no form of the church can be final, short of the kingdom, but it has also contended that the unity we seek must be *visible* in order "that the world may believe."

2. A second well-known concept regards agreement on "the gospel rightly preached and the sacraments rightly administered" as the necessary presupposition of unity. The classic statement of this stance is article seven of the Lutheran Augsburg Confession:

> It is sufficient for the true unity of the Christian Church that the gospel be preached in conformity with a pure understanding of it and that the sacraments be administered in accordance with the divine Word. It is not necessary for the true unity of the Christian Church that ceremonies, instituted by men, should be observed uniformly in all places.

"What is being emphasized here," notes Vischer, "is the sources from which unity can always be renewed: if these are undefiled, then whatever the diversities the Church will be preserved in purity and unity."[2] It is important to note that Augsburg, with its derogatory reference to "ceremonies," has been repeatedly invoked to justify the continuation of confessional identity.

3. A third group of churches sees episcopal structure as being of decisive importance to the realization and maintenance of unity. The church is visibly one when its bishops, as representatives of their churches, are in communion with each other and in continuity with the early church. An expression of this view, one that has had great influence on discussions about the nature of unity throughout the ecumenical movement, is the famous Anglican Lambeth Quadrilateral of 1888 (reformulated as the "Appeal to All Christians" by the Lambeth Conference of 1920). According to this document, unity will require (a) the recognition of the Holy Scriptures as the rule and final measure of faith, (b) the recognition of the Apostles' Creed and the Nicene Creed as the proper declaration of Christian faith, (c) the use of baptism and communion as instituted by Christ, and (d) the recog-

---

2. Vischer, "Drawn and Held Together by the Reconciling Power of Christ," p. 173.

nition of the historical episcopate as the keystone of governmental unity. Roman Catholics maintain, of course, that there needs to be primacy within the college of bishops, a role exercised by the pope, the bishop of Rome, who is the focus of both truth and unity in the church.

4. A fourth concept, often difficult for Protestants to grasp, is that unity is guaranteed by common participation in the true and living Tradition of the church. Orthodox churches in particular contend that through the power of the Holy Spirit, God is always renewing the church in historical continuity with the apostles and the church of the first centuries. "Divided Christians can therefore only find their unity as they let themselves be drawn together into this living and lived tradition."[3] For the Orthodox, such unity would be best expressed through common participation in a true Christian council (in French, *concile*) that, unlike the present World Council (in French, *conseil*), could speak authoritatively for all Christians in the way that the great ecumenical councils like Nicea spoke for the early church. This, too, has had considerable impact on modern ecumenical thinking.

5. The fifth concept mentioned by Vischer is that unity depends less on agreed statements of faith or common structures than on a common willingness to act together, especially in response to human need. This understanding is identified with the Life and Work Movement and its early slogan: "doctrine divides; service unites." As we saw in Chapter III, this concept of unity, while widely held, has never received official endorsement. And many ecumenists today contend that, given the successes of Faith and Order and the furor over the WCC's "political involvements," the slogan should be reversed.

Vischer's list could be greatly extended. I want to mention only one additional concept of unity (perhaps because it is associated with my own tradition, the Disciples of Christ): Unity depends on the recovery or restoration of the New Testament church. All that is necessary for the unity and purity of the church, wrote Thomas Campbell, an early Disciples leader, is that Christians "keep close by the observance of all divine ordinances, after the example of the primitive church, exhibited in the New Testament, without any additions whatsoever of human opinions or inventions of men."[4] That, of course, is easier said than done! We have seen throughout this book that Scripture presents no single blueprint for the church and is inevitably interpreted diversely. Still, churches in the ecumenical movement clearly

3. Quoted by Vischer in "Drawn and Held Together by the Reconciling Power of Christ," p. 173.
4. Campbell, *Declaration and Address* (St. Louis: Bethany Press, 1955).

agree that reflection on the nature of unity must begin with the New Testament witness.

Such wide variation in what unity will require and how to conceptualize it made it impossible for the ecumenical movement, in its early years, to offer a definite model or description of what it hoped to achieve. The WCC's Toronto Statement, issued in 1950, explicitly stated that "membership in the World Council does not imply the acceptance of a specific doctrine concerning the nature of unity."[5] The Council, after all, was attempting to be a fellowship of churches that disagreed precisely at this point. But the Toronto Statement also did not preclude the possibility that the churches would grow in agreement about the character of unity as a result of their "living contact"; in fact, it is the purpose of the WCC to be an instrument of such growth. To be committed to "ecclesiological neutrality" as a permanent principle, wrote Lesslie Newbigin in a commentary on the Toronto Statement, would be to reduce the Council to a debating society and to endorse the present form of conciliar relationship as the permanent, normative form of Christian unity.[6]

Eleven years after Toronto, a new stage in ecumenical discussion was reached—once again by the seminal New Delhi Assembly. We seek to carry the work of the WCC a step further, said the delegates, "not by dictating to the churches their conception of unity, but by suggesting for further study an attempt to express more clearly the nature of our common goal." The result is one of the longest and most significant sentences ever written in the ecumenical movement:

> We believe that the unity which is both God's will and his gift to his Church is being made visible as all in each place who are baptized into Jesus Christ and confess him as Lord and Saviour are brought by the Holy Spirit into one fully committed fellowship, holding the one apostolic faith, preaching the one Gospel, breaking the one bread, joining in common prayer, and having a corporate life reaching out in witness and service to all and who at the same time are united with the whole Christian fellowship in all places and all ages in such wise that ministry and members are accepted by all, and that all can act and speak together as occasion requires for the tasks to which God calls his people.[7]

5. *A Documentary History of the Faith and Order Movement,* ed. Lukas Vischer (St. Louis: Bethany Press, 1963), p. 171.

6. Newbigin, *Ecumenical Review* 3 (Apr. 1951): 252-54.

7. *A Documentary History of the Faith and Order Movement,* pp. 144-45.

Flesh was added to this skeleton by subsequent assemblies, especially the gathering in Nairobi in 1975. "The one Church," it contended, "is to be envisioned as a conciliar fellowship of local churches which are themselves truly united." The delegates saw this not as a departure from New Delhi but as an elaboration of it. A "local church truly united" would have all the marks of a "fully committed fellowship" outlined by the earlier assembly. What is new is the suggestion that each local church "aims at maintaining sustained and sustaining relationships with her sister churches, expressed in conciliar gatherings whenever required for the fulfillment of their common calling."[8] Local churches—with their own cultural, social, political, and historical backgrounds and their own mission focus—"should manifest a rich diversity" (a point strongly made by the 1968 assembly in Uppsala, which called for a "catholicity" that would encompass the diversity of human types and, thereby, serve as "the sign of the coming unity of mankind").[9] But such diversity does not alter the integrity of the one apostolic faith. "Conciliarity," said Nairobi, "expresses this interior unity of the churches separated by space, culture, or time, but living intensely this unity in Christ and seeking, from time to time, by councils of representatives of all the local churches at various geographical levels to express their unity visibly in a common meeting."[10]

These classic statements—of what is called "organic unity" (New Delhi) or "conciliar fellowship" (Nairobi)—by no means answered all questions, but they did begin to limit the range of diverse conceptions. Unity, the ecumenical movement was now declaring, is to be thought of as visible, eucharistic, both local and universal, and involving a depth of commitment signified by the mutual recognition of members and ministers as well as common prayer and service. It will also entail some common confession of faith (rooted in the witness of the apostles) and some common decision-making in regular, representative councils (conciles) at various levels of the church's life (i.e., local, regional, and universal). Such unity also welcomes diversity derived from differences of "space, culture, or time" because this ensures the authentic participation of all human beings in their God-given distinctiveness.

But does unity so envisioned demand the death of confessional identities? There seems little doubt that the dominant opinion in the

8. *Breaking Barriers: Nairobi 1975*, ed. David M. Paton (Grand Rapids: Eerdmans, 1976), p. 60.
9. *The Uppsala Report*, ed. Norman Goodall (Geneva: World Council of Churches, 1968), p. 20.
10. *Breaking Barriers*, p. 61.

WCC, at least through the New Delhi Assembly, was that church unity and confessional identity are fundamentally opposed. The Council had always favored "church union negotiations" between churches of different confessional heritages aimed at creating a national or regional fellowship in which the old identities were submerged (e.g., the United Church of Canada [1925], the Church of South India [1947], and the United Church of Christ [USA, 1957]). And New Delhi, with its apparent emphasis on unity "in each place," probably contributed to an unprecedented surge in such union activity. Between 1965 and 1972, "united churches" were born out of negotiations involving two or more confessions in Zambia, Jamaica and Grand Cayman, Madagascar, Ecuador, Papua New Guinea and the Solomon Islands, Belgium, North India, Pakistan (and Bangladesh), Zaire, and Great Britain. These churches would generally agree with the Nairobi report that union is "costly," entailing "a kind of death," but that "it is dying in order to receive a fuller life."[11]

However, the spotlight was already shifting to a new part of the ecumenical arena. The main factor in the change I have in mind was the entry of the Roman Catholic Church into the ecumenical movement following Vatican II. Since the Roman Catholic Church is global in organization, it looked first for dialogue partners among the world confessional bodies (e.g., the Lutheran World Federation) rather than national-level churches. The idea of union, involving the development of a new identity among churches in various regional or national settings, is much at odds with Roman Catholic ecclesiology. Far preferable, from its perspective, are the bilateral conversations (discussed in Chapter III) aimed at the reconciliation of theological differences between confessional families. These conversations, far from undermining confessional identity, have strengthened it in recent years.

All of this has also led to new thinking about the nature of Christian unity. Perhaps the first major expression of this came in a 1970 speech by Jan Cardinal Willebrands, the president of the Vatican's Secretariat for Promoting Christian Unity. According to Willebrands, unity is best conceived of as a "communion of communions," as a "plurality of types" (in Greek, *typoi*) within the communion of the one, universal church. What does it mean to speak of an ecclesial type or *typos?*

> Where there is a long coherent tradition, commanding men's love and loyalty, creating and sustaining a harmonious and organic whole of complementary elements, each of which

11. *Breaking Barriers,* pp. 65, 63.

supports and strengthens the others, you have the reality of a *typos*. Such complementary elements are many. A characteristic theological method and approach (historical perhaps in emphasis, concrete and mistrustful of abstraction) is one of them. . . . A characteristic liturgical expression is another. It has its own psychology; here a people's distinctive experience of the one divine Mystery will be manifest.[12]

Presumably there is an Orthodox *typos*, a Methodist *typos*, and so on—and these would remain basically unchanged.

A more developed statement of this basic position came in 1974 when, in response to a request by Faith and Order, representatives of the "Christian World Communions" (the various world alliances and federations formed by the confessional families) produced a discussion paper that proposed a new model of "unity in reconciled diversity." This concept endorsed the various constitutive elements for a fully committed fellowship set forth in the New Delhi and Nairobi statements (e.g., mutual recognition of members and ministers, eucharistic sharing, common prayer and service, and joint decision-making). But the paper also announced that "we consider the variety of denominational heritages legitimate insofar as the truth of the one faith explicates itself in history in a variety of expressions." Confessional identities may at times be in error; they must certainly change in response to differing historical circumstances. But, when this happens, they can be "a valuable contribution to the richness of life in the church universal."[13] Through dialogue and shared life, the denominations can lose their former character of exclusiveness, becoming positive expressions of "reconciled diversity."

ARGUMENTS FOR AND AGAINST

The obvious point of tension in the debate, as stated by Harding Meyer, director of the Strasbourg Institute for Ecumenical Research, is "whether not only cultural and geographical (i.e., contextual) differences, but also confessional differences can be regarded as 'legitimate diversities' and thus be maintained in the unity of the church we are striving for."[14] Proponents of "a communion of communions" (e.g., the Episcopal Church in the U.S.) or "unity in reconciled diversity"

12. Willebrands, "Moving towards a Typology of Churches," *Catholic Mind*, Apr. 1970, p. 41.
13. "Reconciled Diversity," *WCC Exchange*, July 1977, pp. 6-9.
14. Meyer, "Models of Unity," in *Vision: Oikoumene* (Washington Institute of Ecumenics, 1986), p. 10.

(e.g., the Lutheran World Federation) argue that they are not backing away from the visions articulated by New Delhi and Nairobi. What they do reject is the idea that "organic union" (such as that in which former Anglicans, Methodists, Congregationalists, Presbyterians, Disciples, and Brethren became the Church of North India) is the *only* valid expression of a "local church truly united." Is there not, they ask, an equally valid alternative model—one in which Lutherans remain Lutherans, Methodists remain Methodists, Catholics remain Catholics, while still participating in a committed, eucharistic fellowship?

Over the past twelve years, several meetings between representatives of "united churches" and the Christian World Communions (CWCs) have helped sharpen the issues at stake. The CWCs, while acknowledging the importance of unity "in each place," tend to emphasize that the one church is a universal fellowship transcending national and cultural boundaries. They argue that the continuation of confessional identities would foster universality by maintaining structured contact among communities with the same confessional heritage. United churches, while affirming that unity must be "in all places," give priority to the embodiment of local fellowship. United churches, their defenders argue, change the basic ecclesial realities with which people live, allowing them to experience and manifest their oneness in such tangible ways that it becomes visible even to their neighbors who are not Christian.[15]

This debate reminds us that there are different types of diversity affirmed in ecumenical discussions. The CWCs have at times depicted themselves as champions of the diversity of theological traditions in contrast to the "uniformity" of structured, organic union. Church union, they contend, may close off theological and ecclesiastical diversity too quickly, producing "remnant churches" of those who, in good conscience, are unable to enter the newly united fellowship. United churches, for their part, maintain that they represent the diversity of cultural settings for Christian community in contrast to the "uniformity" of international confessional blocs. They (especially those from Asia, Africa, and the Pacific) fear that the CWCs export theological motifs (and quarrels) inherited from Western culture that hinder newly united churches from taking authentic root in their settings. The divisions of sixteenth-century Europe, they argue, need not be normative for the worldwide church in this era.

15. See, *Unity in Each Place and in All Places: United Churches and the Christian World Communions,* ed. Michael Kinnamon (Geneva: World Council of Churches, 1983), and especially my essay in that volume, "The Creative Edge."

Along with emphasizing the global character of the church, spokespersons for the CWCs also tend to give much weight to the historical continuity of the church's faith and life, especially as this has found expression in the various confessional traditions. According to this argument, the church is never a "new" entity but lives always in continuity with inherited formulations of the apostolic faith. While acknowledging the need for continuity, united churches give priority to transformation, bolstering their position with three familiar arguments. First, the New Testament speaks positively of the church in different places (e.g., Rome or Corinth) but not of different "types" (e.g., Apollos or Paul [1 Cor. 1]). Second, confessional labels would seem to undermine the Christian claim to be a reconciled and reconciling people, particularly in places where Christians are a minority. Third, those who have undergone union generally testify that, while painful, it has led to enrichment and renewal. As one conference of united churches put it, diversity should be not simply "reconciled" but "creatively integrated"—transformed.[16]

In my opinion, the most eloquent statements of this dispute over the nature of unity are those of John Macquarrie and Lesslie Newbigin. Macquarrie's small book of 1975, *Christian Unity and Christian Diversity,* suggests that

> the best existing model for Christian unity is that which we find in the relation between the Roman Catholic Church and the so-called "Uniat" churches of the East. . . . The uniate relation is one in which there is no attempt to set up a unitary or uniform church, either by absorbing one body into the other or by trying to work out some sort of hybrid. The uniate churches are in full communion with Rome, but retain a measure of autonomy in many areas.[17]

It is particularly important to note, writes Macquarrie, that these churches (what Vatican II calls "Eastern Catholic Churches," Catholic churches that do not use the Latin rite) live alongside the regular Roman Catholic communities in various locations. Thus "the fact that in modern society pluralism is no longer a matter of geography [as united churches tend to argue] has been frankly recognized."[18]

Macquarrie further contends that Christ's prayer for unity (in

16. *Growing towards Consensus and Commitment: Report of the Fourth International Consultation of United and Uniting Churches,* ed. Michael Kinnamon (Geneva: World Council of Churches, 1981), p. 17.

17. Macquarrie, *Christian Unity and Christian Diversity* (Philadelphia: Westminster Press, 1975), pp. 43-44.

18. Macquarrie, *Christian Unity and Christian Diversity,* p. 18.

John 17) "had nothing to do with what nowadays are called 'schemes' of organic union."[19] A single ecclesiastical structure will not ensure the overcoming of division and lovelessness, even as a plurality of structures and names need not deny the presence of genuine communion. Just as marriage demands a combination of intimate union and unique selfhood, so churches need a combination of *rapprochement* and separate identity in their growth together.

Newbigin's response—an essay entitled "All in One Place or All of One Sort?"—regards Macquarrie's proposal as little more than a smoke screen for preserving the status quo, since "it offers an invitation to reunion without repentance and without renewal, to a unity in which we are faced with no searching challenge to our existing faith and practice, but can remain as we are."[20]

Beyond this, Newbigin lifts up at least four objections pertinent to our discussion, objections that, even if they fail to do full justice to Macquarrie's ideas, argue a powerful case for local organic union. First, any model that rests content with present labels undermines mission.

> For how can one invite all men of every culture to recognize Jesus as their one Lord if the confession of his name comes from people who have not themselves found in him a sufficient centre of unity? How will a Hindu recognize the name of Jesus as supreme above every name, if those who bear his name define their own identity not by reference to it, but by reference to the names which evoke the memory of their special religious and cultural histories?[21]

Second, there is a "curious docetism" about any model that dismisses visible structures of unity as secondary or "merely sociological." Human beings need visible, recognizable forms and structures through which to express their love and responsibility for one another. Third, Macquarrie's book reads as if united churches were only an abstract possibility. One "would never guess that more than sixty of such unions have taken place in the past fifty years and that millions of Christians are living in such united churches, daily thanking God for the blessing of unity."[22] Fourth, the crucial question is

19. Macquarrie, *Christian Unity and Christian Diversity*, p. 42.
20. Newbigin, "All in One Place or All of One Sort?" in *Creation, Christ and Culture*, ed. Richard W. A. McKinney (Edinburgh: T. & T. Clark, 1976), p. 293.
21. Newbigin, "All in One Place or All of One Sort?" p. 294.
22. Newbigin, "All in One Place or All of One Sort?" p. 293.

"what form of church unity will correspond to the proper character of the church as a sign of human unity?"[23] As Newbigin sees it, continuation of formerly antagonistic traditions, even if these are now able to share the eucharist and meet in periodic assemblies, is not an adequate foretaste of God's purpose to reconcile all things in Christ. We need a unity that is "welcoming of variety and even contradiction" but also visibly rooted in the saving work of the one Christ. "Such a unity implies the death of all our denominations as we know them. It implies the surrender of every name, every claim to identity, so that the name of Jesus alone may be on our lips, and so that we may find our identity only in the fact that we belong to him."[24]

NEW DIRECTIONS IN CHURCH UNION

Despite Newbigin's hymnic defense, church unions have been few and far between in the past fifteen years. As a result, church union advocates have been led to pursue new and, I think, promising strategies. A quick look at these new initiatives (which, in my experience, are frequently misunderstood) may shed helpful light on the debate over confessional diversity.

Perhaps the major development is the willingness, shown by several different negotiations, to move toward unity "by stages." Several union efforts (in Wales, England, New Zealand, South Africa, and the United States) have established, have tried to establish, or are now establishing "covenants" or other intermediate relationships as steps toward ever more visible unity.

Covenants come in a variety of forms. But, while there is no standard pattern, they have two factors in common: (1) churches entering a covenant agreement need to decide how much unity they can embody now on the basis of what they already hold in common, and (2) they must decide what means they wish to set up for growing together into deeper unity. The plan proposed by the Consultation on Church Union (which involves nine American denominations) calls for a mutual recognition of each other as churches, a reconciliation of ministers, regular eucharistic fellowship (at least four times a year), some common planning and exercise of mission, and the establishment of special "councils of oversight" to facilitate the new relationship. COCU's theological consensus document speaks of the churches witnessing and praying together in their common faith as a way of effecting renewal through the new relationships and commit-

23. Newbigin, "All in One Place or All of One Sort?" p. 305.
24. Newbigin, "All in One Place or All of One Sort?" p. 306.

ments. And all of this works toward "the ultimate achievement of life together in a Church of Christ Uniting."[25]

In sum, a good number of advocates of church union now view it not as an all-or-nothing, onetime achievement, but as a process of gradual growth that allows the churches to strengthen their commitment to each other through interim stages. There seems to be little preconceived adherence to a particular "model" of union (e.g., "the Church of South India model"), but there is an openness to various models since these are seen less as structural alternatives than as different steps along the way toward an ever expanding and deepening fellowship. A good example is the Joint Council between the Church of North India (a united church), the Church of South India (also a united church), and the Mar Thoma Church. For some time these three have had relationships marked by full eucharistic communion, mutual recognition of ministries, common confession of faith, and some common action in mission. Why not move toward "organic union" on the pattern of the CNI or the CSI? In part because the Mar Thoma Church prefers at this point not to let go of its unique identity based on a historical connection with the early evangelization of India. Thus the churches have sought to express what they call "organic oneness" in visible form through a joint council while still maintaining denominational autonomy and identity. It is, proponents argue, an appropriate model for this stage in their common life.

Such examples indicate that there are many ecumenists who, though unwilling to identify "reconciled diversity" with the goal of genuine unity in Christ, now see it as a significant, even necessary step toward such a goal (just as united churches are themselves but steps toward ever broader and deeper unity). Churches involved in union conversations are realizing that of all the reasons for opposing union—fear of compromising truth, a sense that time and effort are better spent elsewhere, ecclesiastical inertia—the primary reason for such opposition is the fear of change and especially the fear of losing a comfortable sense of identity. Covenants and other interim relationships in which traditional identities are retained are seen as good ways of overcoming fears and building needed commitment.[26]

25. See *Covenanting Toward Unity: From Consensus to Communion* (Baltimore: COCU, 1984), and *The COCU Consensus: In Quest of a Church of Christ Uniting* (Baltimore: COCU, 1984).

26. For an overview of these developments, see my essay entitled "Bilaterals and the Uniting and United Churches," *Journal of Ecumenical Studies* 23 (Summer 1986): 377-85.

FINAL OBSERVATIONS

In this chapter I have tried to outline the various positions in what is, admittedly, a complex debate. Now it is time to say where I stand on the issue of confessional diversity. I will make eight brief points. Since these are consistent with the argument of previous chapters, I will not spend much time in elaboration.

1. Confessionalism, understood as fundamental commitment to a particular historically conditioned tradition or as the willingness to be religiously defined by such a tradition, must be regarded as unacceptable. Karl Barth says it very pointedly with reference to individual believers:

> If a man can acquiesce in divisions, if he can even take pleasure in them, if he can be complacent in relation to the obvious faults and errors of others and therefore his own responsibility for them, then that man may be a good and loyal confessor in the sense of his own particular denomination, he may be a good Roman Catholic, or Reformed or Orthodox or Baptist, but he must not imagine that he is a good Christian. He has not honestly and seriously believed and known and confessed the *una ecclesia*.[27]

The Bible, the ancient church (e.g., the Nicene Creed), and the Reformation all affirm that unity is one of the church's fundamental, definitive characteristics. True confession is confession of God in Christ as our only Lord and confession of Christ's one body the church as the single community that bears his name and witness. Fundamental allegiance to a part rather than the whole is idolatry.

It may be argued, of course, that Methodists or Baptists or Catholics can be "reconciled" to other traditions in such a way that they know themselves to be part of a single family of faith. There can be little doubt, however, that in actual practice the confessional traditions often assume such significance for their adherents that our Christ-centered unity is obscured. *To the extent this happens,* these confessions—with their structures, labels, and particular formulations of faith—are, in my view, illegitimate diversities.

2. Denominations, the peculiar form that confessional identity takes in America, frequently reinforce patterns of worldly division. The childhood experiences recounted by ecumenist Paul Crow are by no means unique:

27. Barth, *Church Dogmatics,* ed. G. W. Bromiley, vol. 4, part 1 (New York: Scribner's, 1956), p. 676.

The Methodists were only a block away from the First Christian Church on the square, but beyond their Wesleyan piety
they were rumored to be the church to join if you had execu-
tive ambitions in the local textile mill. . . . The Pentecostals,
unkindly called "the Holy Rollers," were located in the poor
white part of the town. The black churches—Baptist and
Christian Methodist Episcopal—worshipped and served to
God's glory but were in many instances isolated in the ghetto
section.[28]

This may be less true today than it was a generation ago, but to the
extent it remains true, this accommodation of social barriers marks
denominations as unacceptable diversities.

3. Unity needs to find some form of embodied, visible, structured
expression. Genuine unity should never be confused with structural
merger (an imitation of the business world), since true unity rests on
shared faith. But such faith is not simply an inward disposition; it
seeks expression in common worship, common service, common witness—and these demand some form of structure.

Beyond that, unity must be immediately tangible in a way that allows Christians to see that they are responsible for one another in
their "place" and are obligated to make joint decisions regarding their
worship, witness, and service. It may be theologically important for
my father, a faithful member of a Disciples of Christ congregation, to
know that his church is "reconciled" with other Christian traditions,
but such reconciliation will remain abstract unless it enables him to
know himself united through a common structure of action and decision-making with other Christians in his own community.

4. Unity grows both before *and after* the establishment of new
forms of structured fellowship. The experience of united churches
shows that unity falters if there is not sufficient agreement on certain
essential issues prior to union. But it also shows that there are many
problems which can only be faced together once some degree of
deeper fellowship has been achieved. Consensus without visible expressions of commitment is as worthless as (if not more worthless
than) commitment without consensus on basic questions of faith. "It
is not enough," Visser 't Hooft once wrote, "to discuss plans of reunion; we must also expose ourselves right now to those forces
which make for unity, and that means living and acting together on

28. Crow, *Christian Unity: Matrix for Mission* (New York: Friendship
Press, 1982), pp. 7-8.

the basis of the convictions we already have in common."[29] That is one reason why I am excited by the more flexible and dynamic patterns of "unity by stages" now being tried in various parts of the world.

5. Thus far I have come down more on the side of Newbigin and the united churches, but there is much signified by the concept of reconciled diversity that deserves emphasis. For instance, there must certainly be a place for *distinctive* theological traditions in any future unity of the church. Reconciliation will be needed (and has been achieved) on a limited number of previously divisive issues and practices. But Calvinist, Lutheran, Wesleyan, and other theological currents should not be stirred into an approved theological mush because it is precisely the dialogue among such diverse positions that helps stimulate the search for ever-greater faithfulness. However, it does not necessarily follow that there should be communities which identify themselves by the names of these theological currents, retaining separate structural embodiment, any more than there should be identifiably separate Augustinian or Thomistic communities in the one church of Christ.

6. I have already suggested in Chapter II that partners in dialogue need to have a good understanding of their own faith, and, given the present configuration of divided Christianity, this includes knowledge of one's particular confessional heritage, its history and its strengths as well as its limitations. Again, Barth says it nicely:

All churches and all the Christians united in them are called upon primarily to take themselves seriously even in their distinctions and therefore in their separate existence and confession—not necessarily to remain in them, and certainly not to harden in them, but to reach out from them to the one Church. . . . [This] will certainly mean attentively to pursue the intentions of this particular Church to their origins and actual meaning, to try to follow them out, to work out and to put into effect the various possibilities within this sphere, to pay attention and to give voice to this particular witness.[30]

The confessional traditions cannot and should not be ignored in the search for unity. They are an important part of the contexts within which Christians presently live. My argument is not that the confessional traditions and bodies are irrelevant, but that they are sec-

29. Visser 't Hooft, *The Pressures of Our Common Calling* (Garden City, N.Y.: Doubleday, 1959), p. 21.
30. Barth, *Church Dogmatics*, 4/1:679.

ondary to our primary identity in Christ and, to the extent that they obscure this identity, need to be outgrown.

7. It almost goes without saying that no model of unity guarantees that the resulting church will shape its life by Christ rather than the world. United churches, for example, have shown that they can quickly become new denominations, little different from their predecessor bodies.

8. This leads to my last point: The unity we seek is, finally, an eschatological reality—which means that we must always be willing to disrupt our "temporary unities" for the sake of more authentic *koinonia*. (The current ecclesial disruptions caused by the demand for a more racially inclusive community in South Africa and a more sexually inclusive community in Europe and North America are good cases in point.) It is possible, therefore, as Faith and Order said at its 1978 meeting in Bangalore, India, to regard "organic union" and patterns of "reconciled diversity" as alternative "ways of reacting to the ecumenical necessities and possibilities of different situations and different church traditions."[31] Both models are, in a real sense, "interim." Both will require genuine *metanoia* and growth as Christians turn from old patterns of interaction to new ways of expressing the fact that we need and belong to each other.

31. *Sharing in One Hope: Bangalore 1978* (Geneva: World Council of Churches, 1978), p. 240.

CHAPTER VI

THE FUTURE ECUMENICAL AGENDA

Where does the ecumenical movement go from here? Baptism, eucharist, ministry, racism, and confessional identity will undoubtedly remain on the ecumenical agenda for some time to come. But our study of truth and diversity has also pointed to several other concerns that will need considerable thought and effort in the coming years. My intent in this chapter is not to offer a checklist of these emerging issues, but to focus on two that I would like to see receive prominent attention: (1) the teaching authority of the church, and (2) the dialogue between "ecumenicals" and "evangelicals." It is my hope that the understanding of ecumenism presented in this book can help clarify both issues.

BEM AND THE PROBLEM OF AUTHORITY

Authority has been a not-so-hidden concern in each of the last three chapters. Apartheid, for example, has certainly confronted the international church with the question of how it teaches authoritatively. It is not enough to agree in assemblies of the World Council or the Christian World Communions that the theological justification of racism is a heresy. The issue now is how to teach that broad consensus in ways that cause those who practice apartheid to change.

Our discussion of the shape of unity in Chapter V raised the question of where and how such decisions would be made in a future united church. If our unity is to be visible and substantial, said the Vancouver Assembly in 1983, then the churches will need to agree on "common ways of decision-making and ways of teaching authoritatively, and be able to demonstrate qualities of communion, participation and corporate responsibility which could shed healing light in a world of conflict."[1] The concept of "conciliar fellowship" is a useful

1. *Gathered for Life: Official Report, VI Assembly of the World Council of Churches,* ed. David Gill (Geneva: World Council of Churches, 1983), p. 45.

way to envision future decision-making, but many questions remain unanswered. Who, for example, would participate in such councils? It is clear that the ancient councils, in which authoritative decisions about the faith were made (for the most part) by male bishops, do not provide an acceptable pattern for much of the church in our era.

It seems to me, however, that the issue of authority has surfaced even more forcefully in the process surrounding *Baptism, Eucharist and Ministry,* the WCC theological document we discussed in Chapter III. Vancouver observed that "the ways in which the churches respond to *Baptism, Eucharist and Ministry,* and the ways in which they engage in a larger process of reception, provide an ecumenical context within which the churches can learn to understand and encounter each other's ways of making decisions about church teaching."[2] In other words, the theological convergence on faith will now force the churches to deal with the many unsolved problems concerning order.

On one side of the dialogue are those Protestant churches that have found it difficult to make any "official response" to *BEM.* The general board of the American Baptist churches, for instance, acknowledges that "our response has no authority to commit our churches—its authority consists in the extent to which it speaks authentically for them and is received and affirmed by them."[3] How can churches with a basically congregational polity determine whether Faith and Order's work reflects the Tradition of the gospel? Even if boards, commissions, and assemblies express their appreciation for the text, what mechanisms are available for translating that appreciation into ecumenical commitment and action?

On the other side, the more hierarchically structured churches run the risk of having their magisterial authorities issue a response that prevents or undermines real encounter with the text at the local level. Many Catholics and Anglicans were upset when, in the spring of 1982, the Vatican's Congregation for the Doctrine of the Faith released a negative assessment of the report of the Anglican–Roman Catholic International Commission before episcopal conferences had a chance to see that report. Doesn't such action curtail effective dialogue far too prematurely? Doesn't it unnecessarily constrict the community of interpreters?

The questions raised by both of these positions are significant and appropriate. The Roman Catholic Church wants to know, quite legiti-

2. *Gathered for Life,* p. 50.
3. *Churches Respond to BEM,* vol. III, ed. Max Thurian (Geneva: WCC, 1987), p. 257.

mately, how it can move into deeper fellowship with many branches of Protestantism when the latter have few means for teaching the faith authoritatively. How would we know, the Catholics ask, that our unity was rooted in the truth of the gospel? The Protestants, for their part, want to be sure that Catholic hierarchical structures won't blunt the search for truth by absolutizing certain opinions. How would we know, they ask, that our search for truth took proper account of diversity?

Perhaps even more perplexing is the question of what criteria or norms should be appealed to when speaking authoritatively on matters of faith. It is apparent from the American responses that, while the churches are generally positive in their overall assessment of *BEM,* they maintain astonishingly different criteria for evaluating the work or for doing any kind of theological reflection. "The Bible," argue the American Baptists, "is our sole rule of faith and practice," with the Holy Spirit as guide and interpreter.[4] Thus the proper question for Faith and Order to pose is not "To what extent can your church recognize in this document the faith of the church through the ages?" but "Is *BEM* faithful to the witness of Scripture?"

The Lutheran responses contend, as one would expect, that it is not sufficient simply to affirm Scripture as the basis of the church's teaching. We also need a "hermeneutical key" that illuminates the coherence of scriptural truth—and for them that is the doctrine of justification by faith. The Lutheran responses do agree with the Baptist responses that the scriptural era must be the norm for the church's confessions, and they object that *BEM* seems to make certain periods of history normative for faith. By contrast, the response of the National Conference of Catholic Bishops asserts that the church "has always ascribed a specific normative activity to these early centuries," centuries during which the canon, the creeds, and threefold ministry were first given shape. Scripture is inseparable from its definitive interpretation in the Tradition of the church.

The responses of the various American Reformed churches generally add another dimension: namely, an emphasis on the ongoing character of the Tradition. According to the Presbyterian Church (U.S.A.), exploration of the sacraments and ministry should not be limited to the Bible or the first four centuries, but "also should involve the commitment to discern what God is doing today and to take seriously what according to Scripture God has promised to do."[5] In other words, the church is not only traditional but eschatological; it lives (as

4. *Churches Respond to BEM,* vol. III, p. 257.
5. *Churches Respond to BEM,* vol. III, p. 204.

I argued in connection with *BEM*) not only through memory but also through anticipation. Practically speaking, this means taking contemporary experience (presumably with the guidance of the Spirit) as an equal source, alongside Scripture and Tradition, for theological reflection.

Yet another perspective comes from Anabaptist and other free church responses. The Brethren theologian Lauree Hersch Meyer expresses this perspective effectively when she writes that conceptual consensus must be paralleled by concern for existential, historical realities, that an appeal to Scripture and Tradition must be matched by an appeal to lives of embodied faithfulness. The issue, in other words, is not really what the churches say in their authoritative teachings but what the lives of their members actually demonstrate in and for the world. *BEM* goes only halfway. Its concern for the proper content of the faith is of no use unless it enables us to live the reality to which the theological statements bear witness.[6]

Finally, there are certain churches, or groups within churches, that obviously fear the apostolic Tradition as a valid measure of faithfulness to God's will. The Metropolitan Community Church, whose membership is predominantly gay people, acknowledges that *BEM* may well reflect the "faith of the Church through the ages," but "we also recognize that faith to have been a patriarchal, clerical, academic, white, classical, stateist maintainer of the status quo." There is, they argue, a huge counterstream flowing through the ages that knows about woundedness and pain and must now be heard as a basis of the church's authoritative confession. Faith and Order clearly has its work cut out for it as it seeks to make sense of such divergent bases for theological response.

ELEMENTS OF THE FUTURE DIALOGUE

If the "ecumenical problem" is understood as a tension between truth and diverse community, then authority is inevitably a central (if not *the* central) issue. To ask how a church identifies truth is to ask what it considers authoritative. To ask how a church limits diversity is to ask how it teaches with authority. This formulation of the ecumenical problem also makes answers far more difficult. It is one thing to speak authoritatively within hierarchically structured, relatively homogenous groups. It is quite another to work through dialogue and the participatory building of consensus in the context of deliberate di-

6. See Hersch Meyer, "The Church of the Brethren and BEM," *Ecumenical Trends* 13 (Dec. 1984): 161-64.

versity. (This, of course, is what makes the work of the WCC so difficult.) To fix boundaries that divide parts of the Christian family from
one another is to betray the vision I have tried to outline in this
volume. But not to identify boundaries is also to betray this vision,
since the church must be able to oppose the idolatries of the world
with a sure, confident witness. In short, the ecumenical church, in its
search for unity and renewal, must develop a more participatory
teaching authority that lives with the tension between truth and
diverse community; it must insist on the authoritative articulation of
truth (as we understand it) arrived at through dialogue in the broadest
possible Christian context; it must avoid both a weak acceptance of
all diversities and an authoritarian constriction of them.

This question of teaching authority is fundamentally an issue of
ecclesiology: How does the church preserve truth and unity in a way
that is consistent with the gospel it proclaims? Its purpose is ultimately to recall the faithful to their unity of love in Christ and to preserve that unity from the falsehoods that would undermine it. But
questions of authority inevitably involve a host of "nontheological factors"—e.g., fears of losing power and strategies for institutional self-
preservation. This helps explain why authority has not, until recently,
been a major topic of ecumenical discussion. Still, important reflection has taken place, at least on the international level, in three primary settings: (1) in Faith and Order, resulting in a study document
entitled "How Does the Church Teach Authoritatively Today?" (2) in
various bilateral conversations (usually involving the Roman Catholic
Church), and (3) in the WCC's study program called "The Community of Women and Men in the Church." A quick survey of these
three sources indicates several broad areas of agreement on which future work might build.[7]

1. All multilateral and bilateral documents agree that the church
has a responsibility to teach authoritatively on matters of faith. We
have seen throughout this book that, in the words of Faith and Order,
"plurality in teaching is no longer seen by the churches as illegitimate. . . . A new appreciation for the richness of aspects in the Bible
and the vast variety of situations is emerging." But the Faith and
Order document immediately goes on to affirm that "sometimes the
line between truth and error must be drawn."[8] Nils Ehrenström, in his

---

7. For a more detailed survey of these sources, see my essay entitled
"Authority in the Church: An Ecumenical Perspective," *Midstream,* Apr. 1982,
pp. 196-212.

8. "How Does the Church Teach Authoritatively Today?" *Ecumenical Review,* Jan. 1979, p. 87.

1975 survey of bilateral conversations entitled *Confessions in Dialogue,* cites "the increasingly felt need for ecclesiastical structures of teaching and decision-making which . . . serve the upbuilding of the larger ecumenical community now being born"[9] as an obvious case of convergence among the negotiating churches.

Most of the ecumenical texts also note, either directly or by implication, that the exercise of authoritative teaching in the church is not only desirable but inevitable. All churches have a "magisterium," though not all acknowledge such a teaching office or develop it systematically within their structures. The problem with such exercises of authority—whether by seminaries or influential publications or powerful agencies and their boards—is that the larger community may not be involved. The church ends up being guided more by chance than by conscious choice, its doctrinal position determined more by reaction to events than by reflection on them.

2. "All Christians agree," according to the second report of the Forum on Bilateral Conversations, "that all authority derives from Jesus Christ, the Word of the Father made flesh, who is ever present through the Holy Spirit."[10] The church has authority only insofar as it attends to, and proclaims, this living Word. In other words, authority *in* the church depends entirely on the church's recognition of Christ's authority *over* it.

But how is Christ's presence to be known and incorporated in the life of the church? All ecumenical dialogues agree on the centrality of Scripture. But these discussions also indicate (a) that the old view of Scripture and Tradition as separate sources of truth and authority can no longer be maintained, and (b) that there is increasingly widespread belief "in the power of the Spirit to guide the Church into new truth today"[11] (i.e., in contemporary experience as a potential source of revelation). There is also general ecumenical agreement that Scripture, Tradition, and experience are inevitably interpreted in light of contemporary problems and contexts.

3. Who is to interpret? This is where the practical question of authority in the church really begins. And with this question we come to the fundamental sticking point in much ecumenical dialogue. For one group of churches, the authority of right interpretation rests with

9. Ehrenström, *Confessions in Dialogue: A Survey of Bilateral Conversations among World Confessional Families* (Geneva: World Council of Churches, 1975), p. 251.

10. *Three Reports of the Forum on Bilateral Conversations* (Geneva: World Council of Churches, 1981), p. 14.

11. Ehrenström, *Confessions in Dialogue,* p. 250.

a hierarchy of ordained ministers. The Anglicans and Roman Catholics, for example, easily agreed in their bilateral that "in both our traditions the appeal to Scripture, to the creeds, to the Fathers and to the definitions of the councils of the early Church is regarded as basic and normative. But the bishops have a special responsibility for promoting truth and discerning error."[12] This pastoral responsibility may ultimately be rooted in the believing community, but it does not derive its authority from an act of delegation by that community.

For another group of churches, however, authority is grounded precisely in the community itself. Authoritative interpretation in mainline (though not Pentecostal) Protestant churches has usually been governed by the consensus of the church, but the idea of "authority in community" has received even greater attention in recent ecumenical discussion. The Faith and Order study on teaching authority, for example, concludes that "today, there are signs in many churches that more people are participating in decision-making processes." Such participation, the paper argues, "is theologically based on the fact that the gift of the Spirit is given to the whole Church and that, therefore, the discernment of truth needs to take place through the interaction of all its members. Participation is a way of expressing the *sensus fidei fidelium*."[13] This is especially important for women and other marginalized groups that have traditionally been excluded from the authoritative structures of Christian community.

It seems to me that convergence on this issue is occurring because both Protestants and Catholics are recognizing the ways in which they have subordinated *koinonia* to the claims of other elements of the church. If Roman Catholicism has made not the whole church but the hierarchy the authority, Protestantism has frequently attempted to extract the Bible from the church, seeing it as an authority over the church rather than as a manifestation of the church's living witness to the living Word. Most mainline Protestants have disavowed "bibliolatry" by vesting real interpretive authority in representative synods, conferences, and assemblies. And both Nils Ehrenström and the Forum on Bilateral Conversations stress that hierarchical churches are discovering "the importance of the *sensus fidelium* in the learning/teaching church."[14]

I should also note that another part of this ecclesial divide is

12. Cited in *Growth in Agreement: Reports and Agreed Statements of Ecumenical Conversations on a World Level*, ed. Harding Meyer and Lukas Vischer (New York: Paulist Press, 1984), pp. 95-96.

13. "How Does the Church Teach Authoritatively Today?" pp. 87, 88.

14. Ehrenström, *Confessions in Dialogue*, p. 249.

whether or not authoritative decisions can ever be "infallible." The Lutheran–Roman Catholic and Reformed–Roman Catholic bilaterals have both stumbled over Vatican II's assertion that bishops "proclaim infallibly the doctrine of Christ" when, "in their authoritative teaching concerning matters of faith and morals, they are in agreement that a particular teaching is to be held definitively and absolutely."[15] And the claims of papal infallibility proclaimed by Vatican I pose an even greater stumbling block to ecumenical advance. I only want to point out that Protestant wariness of infallibility should not lead to arguments against teaching authority as such. On the contrary, the Protestant emphasis on human limitation and ecclesiastical fallibility would seem to underscore the need for constant and conscious effort in maintaining a continuity of faith.

4. There is general agreement that the community, in its decision-making (however that is understood), should be constantly open to the voice of reason, to theological expertise, to prophetic experience, and to the special authority of those whose lives bear genuine witness to the presence of Christ. Some reports are contending that the testimony of those who have lived at the "margins"—women, the poor, those who are persecuted—has a special authority for the contemporary church. The point is that "authority in community" does not simply mean a democratic vote in hopes that the Spirit is watching; it demands that the community, or its representatives, pay careful attention to the insights of such individual experience and education.

5. Ecumenical documents make it clear that authoritative teaching is far more than a matter of "enforcing" doctrinal agreement. It is better understood as a process of guidance and reconciliation that should not, except in extreme cases, imply sanction or exclusion. The Christian understanding of authority, as exemplified in the life and teachings of Jesus, is not dominating power but loving servanthood. It eschews legalism in favor of sharing, dialogue, and sensitivity to particular human needs. According to the WCC's study called "The Community of Women and Men in the Church," true authority "can never be imposed; it only works when it is offered, chosen and freely accepted."[16] The real authority of a given teaching lies in its "immediate authenticity," in its capacity to convince and, thus, bind the conscience. (Such authenticity stems not only from the apparent truth of the teaching but also from the credibility of the teacher.) It is not sur-

15. "Dogmatic Constitution of the Church," in *Documents of Vatican II*, ed. Austin P. Flannery (Grand Rapids: Eerdmans, 1975), p. 379.
16. Quoted by Kinnamon in "Authority in the Church," p. 201.

prising, therefore, that the process of "reception" in local churches is, as we saw in Chapter III, receiving increasing attention in ecumenical circles. Even decisions made by a broad representative community of the church are ineffective unless there is a "profound appropriation" of them in the life of each congregation.

Ehrenström may sum up the greatest agreement when he writes that "the whole matter of truth-finding and decision-making in the Church is in a state of flux and confusion."[17] This is particularly true, says the Faith and Order study, because "many churches have been led to adopt new forms of teaching in order to provide guidance for their members in their struggle for justice in society."[18] This issue is likely to dominate ecumenical dialogue for some time to come.

THE EVANGELICAL-ECUMENICAL DEBATE

The gap between so-called ecumenical and evangelical Christians, especially in this country, represents one of the new lines of disunity in the church at a time when many of the old lines are being responsibly, carefully erased. Over the past generation, the conciliar movement (i.e., the existence of councils of churches for purposes of common service and, in some cases, theological dialogue) has greatly expanded to include the full range of Orthodox churches as well as the Roman Catholic. The Roman Catholic Church is now an official member of at least thirty-three national councils of churches, two regional councils (the Caribbean and the Pacific), and numerous state councils throughout the U.S. Over the same period, however, those churches identified as "conservative evangelical" not only have refrained from joining but have, in many instances, defined themselves over and against the ecumenical movement and its concerns. As a result, conservative evangelicals are the group most difficult for many ecumenists to deal with. It is curious but true that many leaders of my own ecumenically inclined denomination, the Christian Church (Disciples of Christ), feel greater affinity with the Oriental Orthodox (to take an extreme example) than with the Independent Christian Churches or the Churches of Christ, with whom we share a common historical heritage.

Throughout this study I have insisted that the church must be a community of unlikeness. We are called to serious conversation not just with those partners whose diversities we approve of in advance, but with those who trouble us. This principle has, of course, an

17. Ehrenström, *Confessions in Dialogue*, p. 249.
18. "How Does the Church Teach Authoritatively Today?" p. 78.

enormous caveat: such conversation is possible and appropriate only with those whom we are able to recognize as, in some fundamental sense, "Christian." I have not the least interest in dialoguing with representatives of "identity theology," which, as I see it, is nothing more than racist ideology with a pseudo-Christian veneer. But such judgments are always slippery (though I will try to offer a bit more guidance in Chapter VII), and they are appropriately rare. "Only an ideological bigot," wrote evangelical Arthur Glasser about the WCC's Vancouver Assembly, "could dismiss the speakers as non-Christians."[19] Such recognition is the basis for making ecumenical-evangelical dialogue an important part of the future agenda.

THE CALL FOR PURITY

The very idea that "ecumenical" and "evangelical" could become ecclesiological antonyms is enough to set earlier generations of Protestants rolling in their graves. Richard Lovelace, professor of church history at Gordon-Conwell Theological Seminary, only slightly overstates the case when he bluntly proclaims, "Evangelicals, after all, invented the ecumenical movement."[20] As evidence, Lovelace cites the Great Awakening of the mid-1700s and the Second Evangelical Awakening of the early 1800s, during which an "evangelical united front" led to renewal in a wide spectrum of churches. Lovelace also points to D. L. Moody's Student Volunteer Movement, which was a major factor leading to the Edinburgh missionary conference of 1910, the symbolic birth of modern ecumenism. Prior to this century, the impulse to unity was an important component of most evangelical streams, since a divided church so obviously weakened Christianity's missionary thrust.

When I speak of contemporary conservative evangelicals, I mean that part of the church which, at least in the English-speaking world, is defined by three characteristics: "the Bible [is] its authority, the new birth its hallmark, and evangelism its mission."[21] In other words, they stress the centrality of Scripture as the authoritative written Word of God, the necessity of personal regeneration in Christ through the power of the Holy Spirit, and the importance of inviting people in all

19. Glasser, "Should Evangelicals Cooperate with the World Council of Churches?" *Christianity Today,* 11 Nov. 1983, p. 82.
20. Lovelace, "Are There Winds of Change at the World Council?" *Christianity Today,* 16 Sept. 1983, p. 42.
21. Timothy L. Smith, "An Historical Perspective on Evangelicalism and Ecumenism," *Midstream,* July 1983, p. 310.

parts of the world to an experience of God in Christ and an explicit confession that Jesus is Lord.

But these characteristics alone do not necessarily distinguish conservative evangelicals from ecumenical Christians. While ecumenists may approach Scripture differently, it is undeniably at the heart of the ecumenical movement (the WCC defines itself in its constitution as "a fellowship of churches which confess the Lord Jesus Christ as God and Saviour according to the Scriptures"). The WCC's widely hailed document entitled *Mission and Evangelism—An Ecumenical Affirmation* speaks a good deal about the need for personal conversion. And, while mission is generally seen to include committed opposition to social evil, talk of evangelism (especially "common witness") is frequent in ecumenical circles.

As I see it, the real difference between evangelicals and ecumenicals has to do with where both camps fall on the continuum of truth and diverse commmunity. "The Evangelical," writes the British evangelical G. E. Duffield, "if he is true to the Bible, does believe that the visible unity of all in each place matters, but if truth is compromised, it may be better to remain separate."[22] There is great concern for the "purity" of the church, both in its doctrine and in the discipline of its members. Appeal is made to such passages as 2 John 9-10: "Any one who goes ahead and does not abide in the doctrine of Christ does not have God. . . . If anyone comes to you and does not bring this doctrine, do not receive him into the house or give him any greeting." Such passages generally serve to limit the range of permissible diversity.

An extreme example of this perspective is found in *The Church before the Watching World,* a small volume by the late Francis Schaeffer. I use this example with some misgivings because a barrier to evangelical-ecumenical *rapprochement* is the latter's tendency to confuse the former with fundamentalism—and Schaeffer is a fundamentalist in his use of Scripture. But he is also a popular writer in evangelical circles, one who is often quoted with regard to ecumenism.

Schaeffer does profess interest in the idea of Christian unity. He writes that we need to practice two biblical principles simultaneously:

> The first is the principle of the practice of the purity of the visible church (not the invisible church we join when by God's grace we cast ourselves upon Christ, but the visible church).

22. Duffield, in *Evangelicals and Unity,* ed. J. D. Douglas (Appleford, England: Marcham Manor Press, 1964), p. 94.

The Scriptures teach that we must *practice,* not just *talk*
about, the purity of the visible church. The second is the principle of an observable love and oneness among all *true* Christians.[23]

Behind the second principle is a crucial assumption: that truth is definitely determinable by reading the literal words of Scripture. "We
not only believe in the existence of truth," says Schaeffer, "but we
believe we have the truth—a truth that has content and can be verbal-
ized."[24] Taking the example of the Fall, Schaeffer contends that there
is "no room for hermeneutics here." Rather, the Fall "is a historic,
space-time, *brute fact,* propositional statement."[25] This leads him to
argue, finally, that the real chasms are not between denominations
but

> between those who have bowed to the living God and thus
> also to the verbal, propositional communication of God's
> Word, the Scriptures, and those who have not. . . . If the
> battle for doctrinal purity is lost, we must understand that
> there is a second step to take in regard to the practice of the
> principle of purity in the visible church. It may be necessary
> for true Christians to leave the visible organization with which
> they have been associated.[26]

MUTUAL REPENTANCE

Dialogue between parts of the church where there has been little
must begin with mutual repentance and a mutual acknowledging of
the other's riches. As a Christian identified with the ecumenical
movement, I would like to take a step in that direction with the following four acknowledgments.

1. Ecumenical Christians are frequently guilty of caricaturing
evangelicals, of lumping considerable variety under that single head-
ing. I can hear some of my evangelical friends loudly suggesting that I
have done just that by quoting Francis Schaeffer in the preceding section. After all, there are a great many conservative evangelicals who
do not share his literalist hermeneutic.

One reason for using Schaeffer, however, is that he serves as an
example from the "other side" of the point I am now making.

23. Schaeffer, *The Church before the Watching World* (Downers Grove,
Ill.: InterVarsity Press, 1971), pp. 61-62.
24. Schaeffer, *The Church before the Watching World,* p. 67.
25. Schaeffer, *The Church before the Watching World,* p. 98.
26. Schaeffer, *The Church before the Watching World,* pp. 74, 80.

Schaeffer labels ecumenically oriented Christians as "liberals" and then announces that liberals "make gods which are no gods, but are merely the projection of their own minds." Similarly, he claims that the ecumenical movement "has nothing to do with objective doctrinal truth," but seeks "organizational oneness on the basis of a lack of content."[27] I have had such accusations thrown at me more than once—and I resent them deeply.

And that, of course, is the point. No one wishes to be the victim of half-informed stereotypes, evangelical Christians included. One such stereotype is the notion that all conservative evangelicals are uninterested in social issues or that those who are interested are a modern aberration of historical evangelicalism. Donald Dayton, a member of the Wesleyan Church of America (a "holiness church"), says that he is usually disbelieved when he points out "that my church withdrew from Methodism because of its compromise on the slavery issue, . . . that my church ordained women in large numbers for a century before the recent controversies in the 'ecumenical mainstream,' and so on."[28] The scholarship of Carl Henry and Timothy Smith has clearly shown that Sojourners and Evangelicals for Social Action have strong roots in the evangelical tradition. If anything, the contemporary tendency to limit religion to the realm of private values is the aberration. Ecumenicals must overcome this and other distortions, must become familiar with the history and contemporary diversity of evangelicalism, for closer relations to be possible.

2. Ecumenical Christians, like evangelicals, can be guilty of overbearing truth claims. One example that comes to mind is a theological statement from a group related to the WCC's program on Urban Rural Mission that makes the following proclamation without specific scriptural citation:

> Jesus was crucified by the religious and political powers of his time because he posed a radical threat to their control of wealth, power and privilege. . . . The basic thrust of the Church's ministry is, therefore, quite clear. It must address itself towards the liberation of the victims of the unjust cultural, social, political and economic powers and structures of society.[29]

27. Schaeffer, *The Church before the Watching World*, p. 68 n. 2.
28. Dayton, "Vancouver from the Outside In: An Evangelical View," *Midstream*, Jan. 1984, p. 65.
29. Urban Rural Mission–Christian Conference of Asia, *Theology and Ideology* (New Delhi: Kalpana Printing House, 1980), pp. 12, 14, 15.

This kind of statement (but one of many possible examples), is, of course, neither an acceptable exegesis nor a self-evident truth for many people who identify themselves as Christian. In a sense, this example points us toward what I regard as the World Council's basic dilemma: Is it, as its constitution states, a fellowship of all those churches that confess Christ as Lord, or is it a body that challenges the churches by taking prophetic stands in opposition to oppressive social forces? The answer must be "both," but in my experience there are many among the Council's staff and commissions who emphasize the latter so heavily that unity-in-diversity is made a secondary or tertiary concern. Seldom is there a call for new division (as we heard from Schaeffer), but there is also little urgency in some quarters for restored unity with those of differing social/political perspectives. At its worst, this means that some WCC statements come dangerously close to a kind of works' righteousness which implicitly identifies the boundaries of communion on the basis of social/political commitment.[30] German theologian Wolfhart Pannenberg, a member of the WCC's Faith and Order Commission, speaks for many when he laments that some in the Council "say that the unity of the church must be defined in terms of *agreement* in the struggle to achieve this unity of humankind."[31] It is understandable that some evangelical Christians think that ecumenism has become an alternative orthodoxy of the left wing, that ecumenism means a particular version of Christian truth rather than (as I have argued) a methodology for understanding the truth of God's will.

3. There is much that the ecumenical movement could learn from the regular, substantial involvement of conservative evangelicals. The "Open Letter" from evangelical observers at the Vancouver Assembly (which is strikingly positive in its assessment of the WCC) identifies two areas of disappointment: (a) there was insufficient attention given in the assembly to "the invitational dimensions of evangelism," and (b) too little was said about the spiritual alienation of individuals from God and, thus, about the redemptive dimension of Christ's suffering on the cross.[32] Both insights are needed as the churches strive for greater faithfulness in this era. I am also fearful of what ecumenist John MacKay calls "Protestant nominalism," in which concern for

30. For a full discussion, see my essay entitled "The Church in the World: Vancouver—Guide to the Issues," *Theology Today* 40 (July 1983): 158-67.

31. Richard John Neuhaus, "Pannenberg Jousts with the World Council of Churches," *Christian Century,* 17 Feb. 1982, p. 75.

32. Evangelicals at Vancouver, "An Open Letter," *Midstream,* Jan. 1984, pp. 127-31.

church membership is substituted for an emphasis on vital personal relationship to Jesus Christ.[33] The conciliar churches have much to learn from evangelicals on this score as well.

All of this brings to mind Hans Küng's axiom that "whoever preaches only half the gospel is no less of a heretic than the person who preaches the other half." The ecumenical churches (at least some of them) have tended to say "The lordship of Christ—demand no more." The evangelical churches have tended to say "The lordship of Christ—insist on no less." Both perspectives are needed in the one body.

4. There is room for diversity even on the question "How much room is there for diversity?" The argument of this book—that diverse community is the context for discovering truth—must itself be challenged in dialogue by those who speak more of truth as the basis for real community. James Dunn draws this conclusion from his study of Romans 14:

> The "conservative" who wants to draw firm lines of doctrine and practice out from the centre in accordance with his particular tradition's interpretation of the NT, and the "liberal" who wants to sit loose to all but the central core, must both learn to *accept* each other as brothers in Christ, must learn to *respect* the other's faith and life as valid expressions of Christianity, must learn to *welcome* the other's attitude and style as maintaining the living diversity of the faith. The conservative must not condemn the liberal simply because the latter does not conform to the former's particular canon within a canon. And the liberal must not despise the conservative simply because the latter tends to count some non-essentials among his own personal essentials (cf. Rom. 14:3).[34]

Ecumenicals sometimes treat evangelical resistance to ecumenism as a defect of character or spiritual insight, a result of narrow-minded malice to be outgrown. In the next chapter I will suggest that the ecumenical vision can suffer at the hands of xenophobia, a fear of otherness—but this is a trait found among supporters as well as detractors of the ecumenical movement. Meanwhile, it is important to remember that Christians have often restricted the limits of their communi-

33. MacKay, "What the Ecumenical Movement Can Learn from Conservative Evangelicals," *Christianity Today*, 27 May 1966, p. 20.

34. Dunn, *Unity and Diversity in the New Testament: An Inquiry into the Character of Earliest Christianity* (Philadelphia: Westminster Press, 1977), p. 378.

ties not because they defected from their principles (or had none) but because they adhered to them. Conservative evangelicalism, even in its opposition to ecumenism, must be credited with holding principled convictions.

COMMON GROUND

In my opinion, there are two notions sometimes held by conservative evangelicals (though more often by fundamentalists) that would be utterly incompatible with the "ecumenical vision" of the church. (1) The church has existed, and undoubtedly will continue to exist, with various understandings of scriptural inspiration. But if a person or a church claims to be an infallible interpreter of an infallible Word, then they have precluded the possibility of meaningful dialogue. Indeed, they have crossed over into idolatry. (2) We need to stress the importance of personal conversion and lived discipleship. But the ecumenical movement will always be suspicious of any individual or group that claims to know who has experienced "proper" conversion or who expresses this through "true" discipleship. The church is a community of forgiven sinners who nonetheless remain sinners, ever falling short of that to which they are called. The church, in other words, is not simply the "pure" community of saintly souls; it is also a nurturing community. To make oneself or one's group the arbiter of sufficient conversion (i.e., to insist on "my kind" of conversion), and to restrict community accordingly, is also idolatrous.

Actually, the opposition to idolatry ought to be common ground on which closer relations can be built. Conservative evangelicalism, writes Lesslie Newbigin, is "best understood as a counter-attack against the increasingly explicit paganism of our modern Western societies."[35] Eugene Smith, a former WCC staff member, has similarly suggested that conservative evangelicals, at their best, are "the true monastics of this age," concerned to preserve the faith in the midst of a collapsing and idolatrous world.[36] These statements are intriguing to me because they parallel so closely my own sense of ecumenism (which I outlined at the end of Chapter II). Surely we see here a real basis for common cause as followers of the One who became incarnate, we together confess, as a rabbi from Nazareth.

The corner toward this new relationship may already have been

35. Newbigin, "The Basis and Forms of Unity," *Midstream,* Jan. 1984, p. 2.
36. Smith, "The Conservative Evangelicals and the World Council of Churches," *Ecumenical Review,* Jan. 1963, p. 187.

turned, especially by the overwhelmingly affirmative response of evangelical participants in Vancouver in 1983. The "Open Letter" previously mentioned notes that the assembly was "spiritually refreshing" in its worship, that it gave "unmistakable loyalty to the historical rootage of our Christian faith," and that it was clearly centered, as its theme proclaimed, on Jesus Christ as the life of the world. The "letter" concluded by asking, "Is there not the possibility that evangelicals have not only much to contribute but something to receive through ecumenical involvement?"[37] Donald Dayton was a member of the "evangelical press" at Vancouver. "I am coming more and more to the conviction," he wrote following the event, "that the future relationship between the 'ecumenical' mainstream and the 'non-ecumenical' outsiders is *the* 'ecumenical' question of our time. And I hope that the 'Open Letter' issued at Vancouver can be a step toward a more genuinely 'ecumenical' future."[38]

37. "An Open Letter," p. 131.
38. Dayton, "Vancouver from the Outside In," p. 73.

CHAPTER VII

THE LIMITS OF
ACCEPTABLE DIVERSITY

Throughout this book I have argued that ecumenism is frequently misunderstood, as much by its supporters as by its detractors. There is a tendency, for example, to talk about the ecumenical movement as a series of meetings, documents, and organizations (or, worse, to equate ecumenism with uncritical support for such organizations). There is a tendency to talk about unity as a commodity which, if we were to achieve it, would result in certain benefits. It is my contention, however, that ecumenism is much more fundamental than that. It is nothing less than a way of looking at the world, rooted in Scripture, that stands in dramatic contrast to the "us versus them" mentality of most human societies.

A good way of making this point is to contrast the ecumenical vision with what might be called the "summit mentality" of contemporary American public life. The summit mentality, to caricature it only slightly, runs something like this: We will talk with our adversary not because we might learn something in the process or because we might reach a deeper understanding of our common task in the world, but because it looks good to our friends, and because it is just possible that the other side will accede at some point (perhaps as a result of our belligerent rhetoric) to the demands of our perspective. The purpose of the summit, said one high administration official before the 1985 meeting between Reagan and Gorbachev in Geneva, is to tell the Russians our view of reality, and the success of the summit will be determined by how well they absorb those lessons in the coming months. The meeting was a success, the president proclaimed to Congress upon his return from Geneva, because we got a fresh start without budging on anything significant.

Genuine dialogue is impossible in such an atmosphere because we (speaking now of the United States) have ideologically determined in advance that we are right and they are wrong, or, worse, that we are a "shining city on a hill" and they are an "evil empire." We have defined ourselves by the ways we differ or think we differ rather than by any possible common ground. There is, of course, a good deal of talk in Washington about unity with our allies, but even this, in the contemporary political environment, often means an attempt to mold our allies in our image, to obliterate our differences. Alternative perspectives on crucial issues are frequently attributed either to evil intent—an approach evident in the president's Dallas prayer-breakfast speech, in which he maintained that those who oppose his views on school prayer and abortion are intolerant of true religion—or to ignorance—an approach evident in the president's 1982 statement that advocates of a nuclear freeze are being duped "by some who want the weakening of America."[1]

The point of all this is not to ridicule Ronald Reagan but to suggest, by contrast, the contours of the ecumenical worldview. Ecumenism is a way of looking at reality that refuses to absolutize relative perspectives. It is an approach to knowledge which insists that truth is seldom discovered in isolation but rather through dialogue in diverse community. It is a way of living that dares to think globally and live trustfully with differences in community, not as a result of polite tolerance but on the basis of our common commitment to and experience of the creating, redeeming, and sustaining God. It is an understanding of human society that identifies the fear of "otherness" as one of the greatest and most pervasive evils we face.

Why, asks Jürgen Moltmann, do "birds of a feather flock together"? His answer, while it sounds a bit simplistic, contains a crucial insight: "People who are like us, who think the same thoughts, who have the same things, and who want the same things confirm us. However, people who are different from us, that is, people whose thoughts, feelings, and desires are different from ours, make us feel insecure. We therefore love those who are like us and we shun those who are different from us."[2]

Human beings long for acceptance. What we seek in another person is often simply ourselves in the other. We increase our sense of self-importance by restricting the circles in which we move to those who are like-minded—which is why the sectarian mentality and accommodation to the dominant culture, both of which ecumenism opposes, are flip sides of the same coin. All of this, says Moltmann,

1. For a similar argument, see my essay entitled "Politics and Ecumenism," *Ecumenical Trends*, May 1985.

2. Moltmann, *The Passion for Life: A Messianic Lifestyle*, trans. M. Douglas Meeks (Philadelphia: Fortress Press, 1978), p. 30.

"is nothing other than the social form of self-justification."[3] It is a reflection of deep-seated anxiety about ourselves and, most tragically,
often involves disparagement of or aggression toward those who
threaten this fragile sense of self-worth.

There is a danger in this line of argument—namely, that those
who fail to support the ecumenical movement will be labeled as insecure and lacking in compassion. I need to stress that genuine disagreement over the effectiveness of this movement—its meetings,
documents, and organizations—is certainly possible among sincere
followers of Christ. But I am convinced that the basic ecumenical impulse, the impulse behind this movement (at its best), is a call to compassionate living.

The English word "compassion" stems from the Latin words *com*
and *pati,* meaning "to suffer with." The essence of compassion is the
ability to empathize, to see the world as another person or another
community sees it, to feel the hurts or anxieties or joys of another as
if they were your own. Surely, this is what Paul had in mind with his
image of the body in 1 Corinthians 12:26: "If one member suffers,
all suffer together; if one member is honored, all rejoice together."
Surely this is what Jesus intended when he commanded his followers
to love their neighbors as they love themselves. Such love does not
necessarily mean approving of what the other does or the way the
other sees. But it does demand that we imagine, make real for ourselves, the distinctive inward life of other human beings. It demands
nothing less than the Christ-like attempt to get inside someone else's
skin, an effort that finds its most awesome articulation in the cry from
the cross: "Father, forgive them; for they know not what they do."

Such living runs so counter to "the way of the world" that it
seems almost beyond human capacity. Contemporary American
society, to return to that example, has clearly made competition, not
compassion, the norm. Genuine empathy—the willingness to see
from other perspectives and the unwillingness to split the world into
us and them—is often regarded as a weakness and a political liability.
Yet Christians affirm in faith that such living is possible for those who
live in the knowledge of God's love, a love which, we confess, finds
full expression in the life, death, and resurrection of Jesus Christ. To
live "in Christ" is, as Moltmann puts it,

> [to be] freed from the cramped life of self-confirmation. We
> lose anxiety about ourselves and become open for others.
> Prejudices fall from us as scales from our eyes. We become

3. Moltmann, *The Passion for Life,* p. 30.

alert and interested, we share in life and give a share of life. Then we no longer feel that we are made insecure by others because we no longer need self-confirmation. The person who is different becomes for us, precisely because of that difference, a surprise which we gladly accept. We can mutually accept each other because Christ has accepted us to the glory of God (Rom. 15:7).[4]

I agree with Ernst Lange when he identifies this inclusiveness, this "bias to universality," as the essence of the ecumenical worldview. "Sinners, lepers, demoniacs, Gentiles, enemies—all those whom society expels to the margins, is driven to expel to the margins for the sake of its own stability—are embraced within the community of Jesus' love."[5] Ecumenism involves an attempt, with the help of the Holy Spirit, to expand the circle of our empathy beyond ourselves, our congregations, our neighborhoods, our denominations, and our nations to include the whole creation (the *oikoumene*) which God has called good, and especially to know ourselves linked in a worldwide family of those who confess that Jesus Christ is Lord. It involves an expansion of the imagination, requiring us (1) to imagine the world and the faith as our ecumenical partners see them, (2) to imagine our own commitments as they look to others, and (3) to imagine the church and human society other than they now are—indeed, as God would have them be.

TWO PRINCIPLES

All that has been said thus far in this chapter serves to underscore the difficulties faced by the ecumenical movement. If ecumenism is not fundamentally a matter of rearranging structural alignments but is better understood as a way of looking at reality, then it is to be expected that "being ecumenical" will simply not make much sense to many people. Being ecumenical often involves a painful shift of paradigms. It involves not simply the reconciliation of various doctrinal truth claims but the overcoming of basic human fears.

Difficult as this already is, however, an additional piece is required. Empathy alone is not the whole gospel. In fact, it can lead to a deadening moral relativism. We may "empathize" with the fears that lead certain whites in South Africa (or the United States) to deny the full humanity of blacks; we may "empathize" with the social pres-

4. Moltmann, *The Passion for Life*, p. 31.
5. Lange, *And Yet It Moves: Dream and Reality of the Ecumenical Movement,* trans. Edwin Robertson (Grand Rapids: Eerdmans, 1979), p. 156.

sures that led certain German Christians of the 1930s and 1940s (as well as many Christians in contemporary America) to confuse Christ's lordship with figures and systems that are less than ultimate. But we dare not refrain from denouncing them. Judgments do need to be made for the sake of our witness to Christ. Lines demarcating acceptable behavior and belief do need to be drawn for the sake of the church's identity and integrity. Openness to diversity does need to be tempered by the demands of truth. But how do we draw these lines without succumbing to us-them thinking? In the next few pages I would like to suggest two principles for determining the limits of acceptable diversity in the church, principles that not only are consistent with the ecumenical "bias toward universality" but are derived from it.

1. The first unacceptable diversity is, quite simply, the absence of love. "Love," writes Hans Küng, "must be the rule even in matters of faith"[6]—by which he means, I take it, that no truth can be discovered or adhered to if the discovery or adherence violates the command to love one another. We are to "speak the truth in love" (Eph. 4:15), but Paul is absolutely clear that love is primary: "If I have prophetic powers, and understand all mysteries and all knowledge, and if I have all faith, so as to remove mountains, but have not love, I am nothing" (1 Cor. 13:2). The major manifestation of the gift of God's grace in Jesus Christ is the mutual, binding love of those who receive it: "By this all men will know that you are my disciples, if you have love for one another" (John 13:35). The world will come to believe less by the purity of our doctrines than by the "visible truth" of our community.

But, if such love is genuine, it must also abhor those things that thwart it. Both Gustav Mensching, in his classic text on tolerance in religion *(Tolerance and Truth in Religion),* and Glenn Tinder, in his more recent book on the subject *(Tolerance: Toward a New Civility),* conclude that "we are justified in being intolerant of all that destroys tolerance."[7] Given the primacy of love (a much better word than "tolerance"), we dare not allow it to be subordinated to other principles. Since love is the glue that holds the community together (1 Cor. 13), the nutrient that causes it to grow (Eph. 4:16), the subordination of love (or the denial of its universality) is a denial of the community's very identity. Thus, once the "German Christians" of the 1930s or the Afrikaner churches of contemporary South Africa

6. Küng, *The Church* (Garden City, N.Y.: Image Books, 1976), p. 328.
7. Tinder, *Tolerance: Toward a New Civility* (Amherst: University of Massachusetts Press, 1976), p. 158.

began to exclude certain racial or ethnic groups from their fellowships and tables (surely examples of "lovelessness"), and to justify such exclusion with theological pronouncements as official policy, then the ecumenical movement had no choice but to acknowledge that these groups had crossed the limits of acceptable diversity and were no longer part of the church, the community of dialogue.

2. The second unacceptable diversity is idolatrous allegiance to things that are less than ultimate. For Christians through the ages, this (stated positively) has meant faith in the sovereign God and confession that Jesus—the Christ, the Son of God—is Lord.

In his exhaustive study of unity and diversity in the New Testament, James D. G. Dunn reaches two conclusions, both of which are critical to our discussion. First, the diversity of New Testament witness is so great that we can say with confidence that "there was no single normative form of Christianity in the first century." The New Testament in effect canonizes this diversity and properly serves as "a standing corrective to each individual's, each church's more limited, more narrowly circumscribed perception of Christianity."[8] This conclusion has been echoed in most contemporary biblical scholarship. Raymond Brown puts it concisely when he writes that the church

> has chosen not a Jesus who is either God or man but both; it has chosen not a Jesus who is either virginally conceived as God's Son or pre-existent as God's Son but both; not either a Spirit who is given to an authoritative teaching magisterium or the Paraclete-teacher who is given to each Christian but both; not a Peter or a Beloved Disciple but both. Tension is not easily accepted in ordinary life, and we usually try to resolve it. So too in church history—but because of the church decision about the canon, attempts at simple resolutions of these theological tensions into a static position on one side or the other are unfaithful to the whole New Testament.[9]

Dunn reinforces our first principle when he argues that not only are claims of a single orthodoxy untrue to the evidence of New Testament diversity, but "such 'orthodoxy' is usually the worst heresy of all, since its narrow rigidity and intolerant exclusiveness is a standing denial of the love of God in Christ."[10]

---

8. Dunn, *Unity and Diversity in the New Testament: An Inquiry into the Character of Earliest Christianity* (Philadelphia: Westminster Press, 1977), pp. 373, 386-87.

9. Brown, *The Community of the Beloved Disciple* (New York: Paulist Press, 1979), pp. 163-64.

10. Dunn, *Unity and Diversity in the New Testament*, p. 377.

But, again, this is not the whole picture, as Dunn explains: "For all their openness to new developments the New Testament writers most caught up in the broadening out of Christianity were conscious that *a line had to be drawn at some point*—that there could and should be a wide ranging diversity round the centre, but that a circumference had to be sketched in at certain points and some expressions of Christianity adjudged to have pushed out beyond it."[11] This leads to Dunn's second conclusion: The unifying element amid the diversity is "*the conviction that the historical figure, Jesus the Jew, is now an exalted being*—that this Jesus is and continues to be the *agent of God,* supreme over all other claimants to the titles, Lord and Son of God."[12] In a world filled with idols, in a world where humans repeatedly place themselves in bondage to limited realities, Christianity offers the confession that God alone is the source of creation and redemption and that in Jesus' life, death, and resurrection we see the embodiment of divine grace, wisdom, and power. This conviction, writes Dunn,

> would appear to be the irreducible minimum without which "Christianity" loses any distinctive definition and becomes an empty pot into which men pour whatever meaning they choose. But to require some particular elaboration of it as the norm, to insist that some further assertion or a particular form of words is also fundamental, would be to move beyond the unifying canon within the canon, to erect a canon on only one or two strands within the New Testament and no longer on the broad consensus of the New Testament writings as a whole.[13]

The Jesus tradition is not, of course, uniformly interpreted within the New Testament itself. The canon is able to encompass Matthew, Paul, and John as well as the Pastoral Epistles and the Revelation to John, but it *cannot* encompass Ebionism (which sees Jesus as an inspired prophet) or Docetism (which denies the real humanity and suffering of Christ). The various "Jewish Christian" documents in the canon insist that the historical Jesus, the itinerant charismatic preacher from Nazareth, is truly the exalted Lord, in whom we have a paradigm for our relations with God and one another and to whom, therefore, all obedience and honor are due. And the various "Hellenistic documents" insist that the Christ, the glorified Lord, the

11. Dunn, *Unity and Diversity in the New Testament,* p. 306.
12. Dunn, *Unity and Diversity in the New Testament,* p. 56.
13. Dunn, *Unity and Diversity in the New Testament,* p. 376.

one mediator between God and humanity, is also the man Jesus who suffered an excruciating and ignoble death on a Roman cross. All twenty-seven books—indeed, all sixty-six books—constitute a passionate rejection of idolatry. The one God has drawn near—in the Exodus, in the prophets, in Jesus the Christ—that we may worship and serve no other powers. All other principalities and dominions have been disarmed for those who experience the freedom of God's loving forgiveness in faith—revealed, we confess, most supremely in Jesus Christ. To give ultimate allegiance to anything else (whether that be nationality or economic ideology or personal ego or visions of earthly achievement), and especially to justify that allegiance theologically, is to move outside the circle of acceptable Christian diversity.

TWO OBSERVATIONS

These two principles undoubtedly raise numerous questions; that is as it should be. But I may be able to avoid some unnecessary misunderstandings with the following observations.

First, it must be quickly admitted that most members of the church are idolatrous to some extent, particularly in the way we treat religion as one compartment among many in our lives. When it comes to business, we put our faith in Wall Street. When it comes to politics, we trust in Washington. When it comes to "security," we want to believe in the Pentagon. And when it comes to the care of our souls, we dust off our Christianity—and wonder why our lives seem so spiritually empty and out of control. That is why it is far preferable to speak of repentance rather than excommunication, chastisement rather than exclusion, renewal rather than heresy, reformation rather than division. "Who are you to pass judgment on the servant of another? It is before his own master [i.e., God] that he stands or falls" (Rom. 14:4). We leave it to God to separate tares from wheat "since all have sinned and fall short of the glory of God" (Rom. 3:23).

As we noted in Chapter V, the situation does change when speaking of communities rather than individuals, but even here division should be an action of last resort. In his letter to the Galatians, Paul begins by lamenting that they have turned from Christ "to a different gospel" (1:6). Indeed, in their desire to be justified by the Law they are "severed from Christ" (5:4). And yet Paul addresses his epistle to "the churches of Galatia"; he obviously understands himself to be speaking to Christian brothers and sisters who, though they have strayed from the faith and are in need of renewal through the

Spirit, are nonetheless part of God's church. The emphasis, as I have said before, is on excluding error, not congregations.

Second, the two points made in the preceding section are actually complementary parts of a single principle. Lack of love toward God's creation *is* idolatry, but such love must know its proper source and object. "Diversity," Dunn concludes, "which abandons the unity of the faith in Jesus the man now exalted is unacceptable; diversity which abandons the unity of love for fellow believers is unacceptable. . . . Where diversity meant a breach in love towards those who also called upon the name of this Jesus, then diversity had gone too far. *The centre also determined the circumference.*"[14] Commitment to the lordship of Christ demands love for those who also claim him as Lord.

Robert Jewett makes the same point with reference to the first two commandments from Sinai. He argues that faith without tolerance, without an expansion of our circle of empathy, is a violation of the second commandment. It is, in fact, an act of idolatry, making graven images out of finite definitions. But tolerance without faith violates the first commandment, basing our lives on something other than the transcendent God of Abraham, Isaac, and Jacob. The two commandments must be held together if we are to determine the limits of legitimate diversity.[15]

TO BE THE CHURCH GOD WILLS

Throughout this book I have had two overriding concerns: parochialism and idolatry. I have tried to hold together (1) the importance of being a community that proclaims Christ's lordship with conviction to an idolatrous world, and (2) the importance of being an open community which knows that its knowledge of Christ is never complete and, therefore, that it needs to include people who see from different perspectives.

The problem, as I have previously noted, is that we Christians often act as if these two concerns are mutually exclusive. And, in fact, sociological studies seem to confirm this bifurcation. The main conclusion of Dean Kelley's *Why the Conservative Churches Are Growing* is that "social strength and leniency do not seem to go together."[16] Those churches that are increasing numerically—and

14. Dunn, *Unity and Diversity in the New Testament,* pp. 378-79.
15. Jewett, *Christian Tolerance: Paul's Message to the Modern Church* (Philadelphia: Westminster Press, 1982), p. 69.
16. Kelley, *Why the Conservative Churches Are Growing* (New York: Harper & Row, 1972), p. 83.

whose members display strong, overt commitment and discipline—
are those characterized by "absolutism" (we have the truth and all
others are in error) and "conformity" (deviance or dissent is unacceptable). Meanwhile, churches appreciative of diversity and dialogue
are decreasing numerically (at least in the United States) and often
seem marked by "lukewarmness." Members of ecumenical churches,
in other words, do not seem to feel themselves "caught up in a dynamic movement that shakes them loose from conventional culture,
sends them forth in disciplined mission, at great sacrifice, for the sake
of meaning."[17]

Does it need to be this way? If the church announced in Scripture
is to be an ecumenical community of Gentile and Jew, should we
bow to the logic of sociological analysis? Isn't it possible—indeed, essential—to be both evangelical and ecumenical, both aggressive in
our proclamation and humble in our love? The "public church" (i.e.,
the ecumenical church) seems defenseless, writes Martin Marty, because "most people have not yet learned to put as much passion and
staying power in open-ended religio-ethnic-cultural combinations as
in attempts to form tribes whose members will see all outsiders as
devils. . . . The public church should focus the 'passion for openness'
among its adherents."[18] The search for unity is itself a truth claim, a
response to the witness of Scripture, that should result in firm, active
commitment. Ecumenical Christians should not be embarrassed by
their openness, as if it were a sign of weakness; they should be aggressive ambassadors of Jesus Christ, who prayed for the unity of his
followers (John 17:21), and whose ultimate purpose is the unity of all
creation, in heaven and on earth (Eph. 1:10). It simply does not follow that a certain amount of openness at the boundaries betrays a
vacuum at the center; in fact, the opposite would seem more likely.
We build walls when the center is fragile. We should dare to live in
vulnerable openness when the center is solid.

According to the great biblical scholar C. H. Dodd, "the govern-
ing idea in the New Testament is that of the one Church—a unique
society constituted by an act of God in history."[19] It is unique in that
one becomes part of this community not by obedience to the Law or
circumcision or race or gender or social status or nationality or moral
excellence or wisdom or doctrinal purity, but by confession that the

17. Kelley, *Why the Conservative Churches Are Growing*, p. 86.

18. Marty, *The Public Church: Mainline-Evangelical-Catholic* (New York:
Crossroad, 1981), p. 7.

19. Dodd, quoted by Crow in *Christian Unity: Matrix for Mission* (New
York: Friendship Press, 1982), p. 32.

God of love, made flesh in Jesus the Christ, is the source, purpose, and sustaining power of one's life.

Why is the unity of the church so important to the Christian understanding of reality? Why do I insist that it is linked so definitely to the rejection of idolatry? Because this new unity in Christ, this undreamed-of oneness of Jew and Greek, would be a sign to the world of the reconciling purpose of God and a demonstration of God's power to make it happen. The power of the New Testament church stemmed not from what it did as a small, politically powerless band, but from what it was—a body which, through God's Spirit, united former enemies around the living truth, Jesus Christ. William Stringfellow expresses it beautifully:

> What is to be established is the Church as a living people, a holy nation, manifest and militant in the world, embracing every diversity of mankind, here and now transcending all that separates, alienates, and segregates [men] from themselves, each other, or the rest of creation. The witness of the Church in and to a broken, divided, and fallen world is that of a new society in which worldly standards have ceased to count.[20]

The church should stand as a radical critique of our age and our culture, in which ideological lines are hardening and real dialogue is diminishing in the public arena. It should be an incarnate protest against the us-them mentality of this or any era. In a world seemingly bent on self-destruction, in a world where empathy seems so often confined to members of like-minded enclaves, in a world that appears to live more by fear than by hope, the ecumenical vision of Christ's one body, living as sign and foretaste of God's *shalom,* is not an optional commitment, not a luxury that is conveniently demoted on our ecclesiastical lists of priorities, not something best left to experts on the nuances of theological debate. It is an inescapable and indispensable part of what it means to be the church God wills.

20. Stringfellow, *Dissenter in a Great Society* (Nashville: Abingdon Press, 1966), p. 145.